FACING FEARS, PHOBIAS, AND ANXIETY

Stewart Agras, M.D.

W. H. Freeman and Company
New York

This book was published originally as a volume of *The Portable Stanford*, a book series published by the Stanford Alumni Association, Stanford, California.

Library of Congress Cataloging in Publication Data

Agras, W. Stewart.
  Panic : facing fears, phobias, and anxiety

  Includes index.
  1. Fear   2. Phobias   3. Anxiety   4 Panic   I. Title
RC535.A37   1985   616.85′225   84-4378
ISBN 0-7167-1730-1
ISBN 0-7167-1731-X (pbk.)

Printed in the United States of America
2 3 4 5 6 7 8 9 0   ML   4 3 2 1 0 8 9 8 7 6

CONTENTS

ACKNOWLEDGMENTS

The unsung heroes of this book are the patients who have generously donated their time to the research projects conducted in my own laboratory and in the laboratories of my colleagues at Stanford and elsewhere. Many of these phobic individuals have provided me with valuable insights into their condition, and in the aggregate they have helped advance both our basic understanding of the nature of fear, phobia, and panic and the development of more effective treatment. The health care enterprise and the biobehavioral sciences could not flourish without the help of research volunteers. I am deeply indebted to them all, as are all those future victims of fears, phobias, and panic who will benefit from the new levels of understanding and treatment that these volunteers have helped to establish.

The community of scientists working on these disabling conditions is large and far-flung; valuable studies have come from many countries and I have drawn on their findings in the making of this book. I have also had the opportunity to refine my ideas in conversations with colleagues from many centers in the United States and other countries. There will, I believe, be general agreement with many of the propositions put forward here, although there will also be disagreement with some of the details. In writing this book, I have attempted to present a coherent picture of the current understanding of the causes and treatment of fears, phobias, and panic in what is, I hope, a useful format for the interested general reader, the sufferer, and the student.

In its making, a book is shaped by many hands. I would like to thank the staff of The Portable Stanford for the many valuable suggestions that have enhanced this book. In particular, I would like to thank Miriam Miller for her unstinting help in improving its readability—a task that the word "editing" barely describes.

Stewart Agras

Stanford University
April 1985

THE TERRITORY OF FEAR 1

Even the bravest among us have experienced fear at one time or another, though we may not like to remember such experiences. The sudden scare at the sight of a harmless snake, the sweaty palms and racing heart on takeoff or flying through bumpy air, or the dry mouth and constricted throat before beginning a speech—all are symptoms of fears or phobias. Our fears limit us, sometimes in small ways, sometimes in ways so large that we become imprisoned by them. Often the shame of exhibiting a weakness inhibits us from talking about, exploring, and mastering our fears, and thus encourages accommodation to a limited state of being and to a lesser degree of freedom than life should afford.

One of the aims of this book is to examine what we know about panic, fears, and phobias in order to make these common occurrences less mysterious and to provide a clearer picture of ourselves. Acknowledging and confronting our fears can diminish them and eventually cause them to disappear, reducing our limitations, lessening our anxiety, and, for some, leading to a profound liberation.

We will explore the territory of fear as we understand it today—from the slightest startle at an unexpected sound, through common experiences such as shyness or a fear of airplane travel, to the extreme disability associated with the full-blown panic disorder. Although fear is an integral, and even useful, aspect of the human experience, it is always accompanied by a restriction of action. When fear gets out of hand and becomes an illness, it may markedly restrict one's life; irrational fears keep untold numbers of people from reaching their full potential.

We will not deal in this book with realistic fears, such as those shared by city dwellers for centuries—fears of burglary and muggings, robbery and beatings. Instead, we will explore the less rational side of human nature—those aversions which, although subjectively experienced as very real and often terrifying, are objectively regarded as unrealistic. Our exploration will encompass fears of objects and situations that do not pose a physical threat, at least to adults—fears that we often keep hidden even from those close to us.

■

Before proceeding with our exploration, let us take a moment to define more precisely what we are talking about. Fears that are widely shared are referred to as *common fears*. Although a sudden encounter may cause anxiety, the feared object or situation can be faced in the ordinary course of everyday life; and while such a fear may result in some limitation of action—for example refusing to walk in tall grass for fear of encountering a harmless snake—the degree of disability is small.

The critical distinction between a common fear and a *phobia* is the degree to which it interferes with everyday life. Although a fear of a harmless snake may be intense, or may extend to a fear of crawling insects and mice (when moving quickly, mice evoke a visual pattern much like a snake), such a fear is not likely to interfere much with everyday living. So a fear of harmless snakes is rarely considered a phobia. On the other hand, a fear of heights, if accompanied by avoidance of offices on the top floors of high buildings, of high-rise hotels, or rooftop restaurants, will interfere with work or leisure activities, and in that case may be considered a phobia.

Take, for example, the celebrity who has come to give a witty and urbane speech, delivered it with confidence, and now must travel a thousand miles or more by train to get home because of a fear of flying. Here is a phobia that creates a severe limitation in an otherwise successful person's life.

A *simple phobia*, then, involves a single object or situation, such as small animals, enclosed places, or thunderstorms. Phobics will go out of their way to avoid such objects or situations, and if they encounter them, they will flee at the earliest possible moment. In addition, the phobic will anticipate such encounters with great anxiety. The borderline between a severe common fear and a mild simple phobia is not clearly demarcated; the distinction depends to some extent upon the individual's perception of the affliction and whether he or she feels inconvenienced enough by the phobia to seek treatment.

A *panic attack* is an intense burst of anxiety accompanied by marked physiological uproar and many strange changes in bodily feelings. Attacks may last from a few minutes to a few hours, and each attack will leave the victim feeling shaken and exhausted. Some of these attacks come out of the blue, others occur within a phobic situation and are therefore not entirely unexpected. Because panic attacks are not associated with a simple phobia, we will use the term *panic syndrome* to describe the affliction characterized by repeated panic attacks. Sometimes these afflictions remain unchanged in their severity for many years and are marked by several panic attacks a week. At other times the symptoms wax and wane, often for no discernible reason. Perhaps more frequently, the repeated experience of panic eventually leads the sufferers to so restrict their activity that they reach a condition known as *agoraphobia*, literally "fear of the marketplace," a disability that may eventually result in their becoming completely housebound.

We will refer to phobias accompanied by panic attacks as *complex phobias* for two reasons: First, the combination of panic and phobia is usually more disabling than a simple phobia, and second, the disorder is often characterized by multiple phobias. Thus the agoraphobic may not only be housebound but may also suffer from *claustrophobia* (fear of enclosed places), *acrophobia* (fear of heights), and injury and illness phobias, sometimes referred to as *hypochondriasis*. *Social phobia*, the fear of entering social situations, may range from simple shyness at one extreme to an avoidance of most social encounters at the other, and may also be accompanied by panic attacks. Hence this disorder may be classified as a simple phobia in some circumstances, and a complex phobia in others. *Compulsions* may further complicate certain types of phobias. These are repetitive rituals that the sufferer feels compelled to engage in as a means of avoiding a feared consequence, such as becoming ill or harming others. This condition is extremely disabling, since so much of the victim's time is taken up with performance of the rituals. Luckily, it is also the rarest of all these disorders.

■

The common fears, phobias simple or complex, the panic syndrome, and compulsive behavior pose a fascinating research and treatment challenge that is gradually being conquered. While fears and phobias have undoubtedly remained relatively unchanged for centuries, the scientific exploration of these phenomena, apart from early philosophical speculation, only began at the turn of this century. Since, as we shall see in Chapter 3, the common fears are so ubiquitous, they must have a function. The thesis that we will explore in this book is that the common fears are a biological implant aimed at protecting the young against possible injury, that fear becomes a nursemaid as the young leave their mother's side and begin to explore their world. These fears disappear as we grow up and can better look after ourselves, although, as we shall see, most adults retain some vestiges of fear throughout their lives. The argument to be developed suggests that phobias emerge from the remnants of common fears, which, instead of disappearing, become prolonged and intensified.

Not only will we explore the reasons thought to underlie the prolongation of fears into phobias, but we will also investigate what is known about the processes underlying fear and avoidance behavior at three levels: observable behavior, physiology, and chemical processes within the brain. It is often said that psychology, the study of behavior, will ultimately be replaced by the neurosciences as we come to better understand the electrochemical changes that occur within the brain as we think and act. Such a reductionist view would, however, suggest that quantum physics might ultimately explain behavior. Another point of view informs this book: that different levels of explanation can be linked one to another, but that the laws governing each level are different and therefore not reducible to a more "basic" level. Understanding the chemical workings of the brain will not result in better counseling for the phobic; to fulfill that function, a better understanding of the rules governing behavior change is needed.

Later in the book we will trace the development of treatment strategies for the various conditions of interest to us, showing how the field has progressed from relatively nonspecific treatment approaches such as psychotherapy to a more precisely directed attack, which more often leads to a resolution of fears and phobias. Similarly, the development of effective pharmacological approaches to the treatment of these disorders will be examined, so that we can see how these two different approaches, psychological and pharmacological, must be applied in different combinations in the treatment of simple phobia, panic, and the complex phobias. This is one way in which the fields of psychology and neurobiology can usefully relate to each other.

While some of the disorders we will examine are profoundly disabling, others are mere nuisances; yet they all limit our behavior and keep us from developing our full potential. Luckily, the psychological principles underlying the treatment of complex phobias can readily be applied in simpler form to the eradication of common fears, and we will find that there is much that phobics can do to help themselves.

THE DESCENT OF PANIC 2

"**F**inally, they reached a stairway where the fleeing mob funneled almost to a standstill. Panic exploded as passengers fought for a chance to live. Men struggled unheedingly past women and children; one woman pushed aside a frightened little child. The only possible way up the stairs was to grasp the stairway railing and hold on determinedly. The polished bar became a desperate prize."[1] This is the kind of scene we usually associate with the word "panic"—an acute reaction to catastrophe shared by a group of people—in this instance, passengers aboard the *Andrea Doria*, the Italian ship rammed off the coast of the United States by the liner *Stockholm*. The description is by one of the survivors who was trying, with his fellow passengers, to reach the comparative safety of an upper deck of the steeply listing luxury liner.

Panic as a reaction to catastrophe is in fact quite rare. The most common experience of panic is that which suddenly descends upon an unsuspecting person, turning an ordinary day into a terrifying and bewildering experience vividly etched upon the memory as the beginning of a strange and often long-lasting illness—an illness that, because of the constant fear of a sudden and unforeseen panic attack, may lead to an increasing limitation of activity that we call phobia. Full-blown, it is a cruel illness, virtually imprisoning its victims within their homes.

Since no one is fearless, or entirely free of anxiety, everyone can empathize with the experiences that characterize the onset of panic. Imagine that you are walking along a busy street. Perhaps it is a hot day and you feel a little tired. People jostle by. Drivers honk their horns. You usually ignore these noisy intrusions. But today they seem to press in on you. You feel irritable, perhaps resentful, toward those who crowd you.

As you walk along, you become aware of a strange feeling in your chest, a tightness or a dull pressure. You try to ease this feeling by breathing more deeply, but it seems difficult to fill your lungs with air. You feel a little sick and begin to wonder what is wrong. Then you notice that your heart is beginning to speed up and beat irregularly. Perhaps you feel both feverish and sweatily cold at the same time. Now things around you seem to fade away one moment and become overly bright the next. Noises press in on you.

If this happened to you, what would you think was wrong? A heart attack? Influenza? Indigestion? Perhaps you would think you were going insane. With these symptoms, any of these explanations might be correct.

Continue to imagine: As thoughts of heart attack and insanity flash through your mind, the symptoms become worse. Now you feel restlessness and a desire to rush home, or perhaps you have a feeling that you are going to die. You remember that a relative or a friend recently died of a sudden heart attack. As you concentrate on the peculiar feelings in your chest, your heart speeds up even more and the beat feels more irregular. Your breathing becomes labored. Nothing you do helps. Even when you get home and lie down you feel just as bad.

Eventually the attack subsides, and you feel almost normal. What a relief, perhaps it is all over! But in a day or two, another, perhaps worse, attack occurs. Sooner or later you want to find out what is wrong. You visit your doctor. But your doctor finds nothing. You suspect that something has been missed, that you are the victim of an undiscovered mental or physical disease. In fact, you may be experiencing the onset of the panic syndrome.

■

The panic syndrome is a distinct psychophysiological disorder that has only recently been recognized as such. In a recent large-scale survey of three cities in the United States, panic was found to affect 1.5 percent of the adult population. Moreover, the closely related phobic disorders—irrational fears experienced at an intensity that interferes with the normal conduct of life—were the second most common psychological problem in men, exceeded only by alcoholism and drug abuse, and were the most common in women.

The symptoms of panic are so markedly physical that in the eighteenth century the disorder was termed "hysterical vertigo," to describe the sensations of dizziness often reported by the patient. Even as recently as twenty years ago, such incidents were often regarded as fainting spells. Here is a description from the mid-1960s: "A lawyer came to therapy for what was described as a fear involving court appearances. While defending a client, he experienced a sudden, rapid rise in pulse, with a fear of fainting, and was forced to leave the courtroom. . . . The patient thought he was having a heart attack, and for a great many years was preoccupied with his cardiac state."[2]

The author of this report, an eminent psychiatrist, accepted the description of the event as primarily physical—as a fainting spell. Today, however, this so-called fainting spell would be recognized as a panic attack.

The panic attack itself is only part of what for simplicity's sake we will refer to in this book as the *panic syndrome*. The syndrome includes anxiety, phobia (particularly the limitation of mobility known as agoraphobia), isolation, and depression. The details and extent of the development of the panic syndrome vary from person to person. The broad outlines are, however, surprisingly consistent. Several consecutive stages are typical.

A loss or separation. A loss or separation often precedes the illness. People who suffer from the panic syndrome tend to have been more attached than usual to their families. Many have a history of school phobia, which is more a fear of leaving home and of separating from mother than a fear of going to school. As children they may have been reluctant to stay with friends overnight, or again they may have had fears of sickness and dying, which in the child's mind may represent fears of a separation from family and friends. When these children reach adulthood, a separation caused by the death of a friend or close relative, or by the breakup of a marriage or a friendship, may precipitate the first panic attack.

The panic attack. The first panic attack is often much like the scene described at the beginning of this chapter. It usually occurs in a public place. The victim of the attack suddenly feels ill, notices a fast and erratic heartbeat, experiences a tight feeling in the chest, breathes rapidly, and may feel faint. The rapid breathing leads to chemical changes that cause tingling in the hands and feet, numbness around

the mouth, and dizziness. Nausea, headache, and stomach cramps may also occur during the attack. Often the physical symptoms are accompanied by a fear of death or impending doom, of becoming insane, or of losing control. The victim wants to rush home. Feelings of unreality, such as the sensation of being outside one's body, or of peculiar changes in the quality of light, may occur.

Most victims of panic suspect a physical disorder and seek a medical examination after either the first or subsequent attacks. These examinations rarely reveal any physical problems that could account for the dramatic experience of the panic attack. Because of the discrepancy between the intensity of their experience and the failure of a physician to find any significant disorder, they often become convinced that the doctor has made a mistake and that they are suffering from some serious but hidden physical disorder.

Limitation of mobility. After the first few attacks of panic, perhaps viewed as a temporary illness, a long period with no further symptoms may begin. Then another series of attacks occurs, often more intense, longer lasting, and more frequent than those comprising the first episode. Once more there is a search for a cause and many visits to physicians. After one, two, or even more bursts of attacks, a new feature emerges: Gradually a limitation of mobility develops. At first this limitation may be no more than a mild discomfort in thinking about driving alone on a long trip—one might have a panic attack. But soon a more severe limitation occurs: The patient begins to avoid the places where such attacks have happened. Since attacks may occur anywhere, before long even the thought of leaving home unaccompanied arouses fear. This aspect of the disorder is called *agoraphobia*. In fact, it is a fear of leaving a safe situation. Agoraphobics may also be afflicted with other phobias, such as a fear of heights, of enclosed places, and of eating in public.

Anticipatory anxiety. Panic attacks are not the only manifestation of anxiety experienced by such patients, or even the most frequent. These attacks usually occur only a few times a week. More pervasive is the anxiety aroused by the anticipation of reentering the places where panic attacks have occurred. Such anticipatory anxiety erupts at the first mention or thought of such an outing. Soon anything that requires leaving home may become anxiety-provoking, being fearfully anticipated for many days—a constant nagging worry enlivened by more intense bursts of anxiety.

FIGURE 2-1
The Usual Relationship of Heart Rate to Activity Level

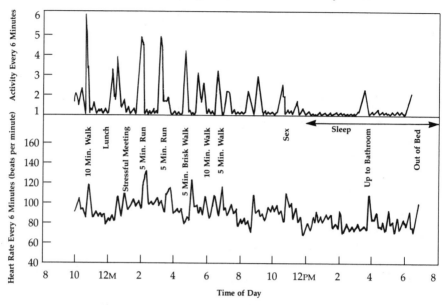

With the actual approach to the feared situation, anxiety may worsen. Such high levels of anxiety may cause a further complication, namely the provocation of a panic attack. Thus, the worst fear has come to pass: Going out has provoked the very thing the patient feared most.

In the most severe cases, being alone even at home provokes fear, and the extent of fear may be enormous. To feel safe, these people must have someone with them at all times. One patient, for example, was so fearful of being alone that she tried to prevent her husband from leaving for work by holding on to him. When this failed, she leaped onto the back of his automobile as he drove off and could not be pried loose.

Isolation and depression. As the disorder comes into full bloom, the enforced isolation of the agoraphobic becomes an imprisonment. This in turn leads to depression that deepens as time goes by. The feeling of being unable to control the panic attacks is a particularly crippling aspect of the disorder, pushing the individual into an increasingly passive acceptance of the symptoms and accentuating the feeling of helplessness in the face of a mysterious illness.

Advanced technology now allows us to examine the occurrence of panic attacks in the real world. Not so long ago, the only way to examine physiological processes was by means of large recorders located in the laboratory. Since panic attacks are not very frequent in a controlled situation, the chance of capturing the physiology of the attack was small. Now, with the development of miniaturized electronic circuitry, lightweight recorders attached to the body can be used for days at a time, with little inconvenience to patients as they go about their everyday lives. The recording duplicated in Figure 2-1 shows part of a normal person's physiological activity during a day and night while wearing the device. One thing is immediately striking. Low activity, say at night, is associated with low heart rates, while high activity, for example while exercising, is associated with high heart rates. The level of activity is a major determinant of heart rate.

When a patient experiencing panic attacks wears this device, a different picture emerges. There are times when, although activity is low, the heart rate is high. These are the times of panic. The attack recorded in Figure 2-2 was triggered by a telephone call during which the patient was told of the death of a distant relative. As the conversation proceeds, her heart starts to beat more and more quickly, until it reaches almost 160 beats per minute, double the normal rate. Yet activity is low. No matter what the patient does over the next hour or two, there is no change. Attempts to relax produce no effect. Only slowly does the rapid heartbeat subside, leaving the patient feeling shaken and still frightened.

A recent study in which this body recorder was used found that during a panic attack, which typically lasts for twenty minutes, the heart rate is raised by nearly forty beats per minute. Contrary to many patients' perceptions that their heart is beating both fast and irregularly, no major disturbances in cardiac rhythm were found. The onset of the typical attack was abrupt, taking only a minute or so to reach maximum heart rate. Interestingly, nearly one attack in five occurred at night, usually between 1:30 and 3:30 A.M., apparently waking the patient from sleep. Are such events provoked by dreams? Few patients report frightening dreams preceding such an attack. These sleep-disrupting attacks may be the purest form of panic, often referred to as "spontaneous panic attacks" and thought to be caused by biological perturbations—a subject to which we will return in a later chapter.

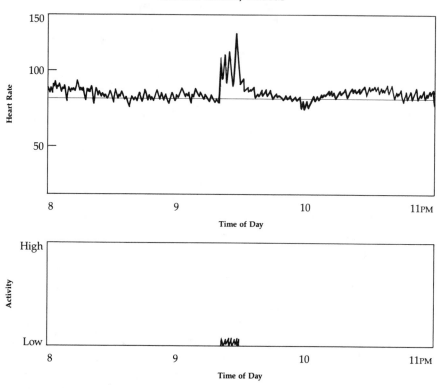

FIGURE 2-2
A Panic Attack, 9:20 PM

The study also revealed that the higher the heart rate, the longer the duration of the attack and the greater the number of physical symptoms reported by the patient.

Some normal persons, that is, persons with no history of panic attacks, were also monitored in this study. Only on one occasion was a panic attack, as defined by a steep and prolonged rise in heart rate, found in this sample. This attack occurred when a woman working on a suicide prevention line received her first call. She reported feelings of anxiety but, unlike victims of the panic syndrome, had no other abnormal bodily sensations. Yet her panic attack was indistinguishable physiologically (to the monitor) from those of the patients. The normal (rationally justifiable) experience of panic induced by extreme stress and the spontaneous panic attack are closely related psychophysiological events; they differ in that one occurs in response to an environmental stress, and the other may occur without apparent reason, and is thus far more terrifying.

The rapid heartbeat that characterizes the panic attack, combined with the physical symptoms of panic, leads many patients to fear that they may have heart disease. While most of these fears are unfounded, some physicians have suspected that there may be a connection between anxiety and actual heart disease. During the American Civil War, a doctor reported hearing "clicks and murmurs" in the hearts of soldiers suffering from exhaustion and anxiety. Nearly fifty years later, toward the end of World War I, another physician relabeled this association of exhaustion, anxiety, and cardiac findings "soldier's heart." These observations in men, perhaps exaggerated due to the exigencies of war, were later to prove atypical; it is in young women that the most striking association between cardiac findings and anxiety is to be found today.

Opinion as to whether the physical findings in "soldier's heart" were indicative of real heart disease, or whether they were temporary secondary effects of anxiety exaggerated by the preoccupation with minor sensations in the chest, varied considerably. In the United States, the syndrome tended to be regarded as a cardiovascular problem, while in England it was viewed as a cardiac neurosis often aggravated by the interest of physicians in the symptoms.

The advent of echocardiography has added new information and further controversy. Echocardiography allows the inside of the heart to be visualized without an invasive procedure. The simplicity of the new technique has led to its widespread use and to the discovery that about 10 percent of the population have an abnormality of one of the valves separating the chambers of the heart—a condition known as mitral valve prolapse. In this condition, the mitral valve, shown in Figure 2-3, does not close neatly; instead it protrudes into the left atrium, one of the chambers of the heart, thus interfering with the heart's ability to empty when it contracts.

The symptoms associated with mitral valve prolapse are chest discomfort or pain, palpitations, breathlessness, and anxiety—often somewhat hypochondriacal in nature. Both clicks and murmurs may be heard while listening to the heart. However, many persons diagnosed on the basis of echocardiography as having the disorder have few symptoms and no other signs of heart disease. The sophisticated test may be picking up a simple and harmless disproportion between the size of the valve and the opening between the cardiac chambers.

FIGURE 2-3
Mitral Valve Prolapse

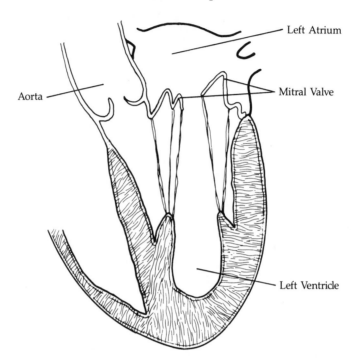

In other cases, however, there is thickening of the valve due to a number of disease processes.[3]

The attempt to determine whether the cause is a diseased valve or a normal variant is often complicated by the role of anxiety in producing signs that may mimic the disorder. For most people, a consultation with a cardiologist is in itself somewhat anxiety-provoking. For a person who has a lower threshold for anxiety than normal, such an examination may become a major stressor, provoking the finding of more physical abnormalities on cardiac examination. On the other hand, it is also possible that patients with mitral valve prolapse are more sensitive to stress than those without the disorder. For example, various hormonal changes typical of the stress reaction have been described in persons with genuine mitral valve prolapse.

The key question, Do patients with the panic syndrome show more mitral valve prolapse than controls? is still under active investigation. Some studies show an association; others do not. If all the existing studies are combined, we find that 40 percent of patients with panic have mitral valve prolapse as against only 10 percent of controls. This is a statistically significant difference.

An association between a cardiac disorder such as mitral valve prolapse and panic suggests that some cases of the panic syndrome may be due to a biologically induced multi-system disease. A recent study found that minor skeletal abnormalities (and in the female, small breasts) were associated with mitral valve prolapse. All these tissues, including the mitral valve, develop simultaneously, and from the same source, in the embryo, and a chemical abnormality might easily affect their development in very early life. It is also possible that tissues in the central nervous system could be affected at the same time, which would explain the conjunction of mitral valve prolapse and panic disorder. Such findings and speculations form one line of evidence for the biological underpinnings of this common disorder. However, since mitral valve prolapse occurs in a minority of those suffering from panic, such an explanation would account for only a fraction of the cases.

Long-term studies demonstrate a higher mortality rate for persons suffering from neuroses (anxiety-based disorders) of all types than for normal persons. Recent observations suggest that this excess mortality may be almost entirely accounted for by the increased risk of death associated with a single group—persons with panic disorder. Among those suffering from the panic syndrome the death rates due to circulatory disease (heart disease and stroke) were about double the expected rates, while deaths from cancer, a disorder unlikely to be affected by anxiety, occurred at the rate expected for the general population. This indicates that the higher mortality rate in panic patients is due to a single cause—an excess of cardiovascular deaths.

An earlier study had shown that patients with anxiety disorders were more likely to develop high blood pressure than normal subjects (control groups), and furthermore that their high blood pressure developed after the onset of the anxiety disorder. Since high blood pressure is a risk factor for a number of circulatory diseases, the findings of these studies are mutually reinforcing.

Experiments also suggest that animals with a more reactive cardiovascular system, such as would characterize humans with panic, tend to show more damage to their arteries than do their less reactive peers. We must emphasize here, however, that the added risk of death for such persons is small. For these damaging effects of panic on the cardiovascular system to occur, other behaviors may have to contribute

TABLE 2-1

Expected and Actual Causes of Death
in Patients with Panic Disorder

	Expected	Actual
Circulatory Disease	7.4	15.0
Cancer	3.1	3.0
Suicide	1.63	7.0

Sources: Adapted from Coryell et al., "Excess Mortality in Panic Disorder," *Archives of General Psychiatry* 39, 1982.

to the risk of cardiovascular damage—cigarette smoking, overconsumption of unsaturated fat, and a sedentary life style, for example. It is also possible that the rare complication of mitral valve disease adds fractionally to the toll.

■

The mental and physical suffering associated with the panic syndrome cannot be exaggerated. As one patient put it, "Even though I have suffered from physical pain, I had no idea what suffering entailed until I developed agoraphobia." Beyond the acute terror of the panic attack, the anxiety aroused by the mere thought of having to leave home alone or of confronting other feared situations is pervasive and may last for days, and the gradual imprisonment that is the outcome of the phobic avoidance is both limiting and depressing. Not only is the sufferer's working life threatened, but even the simplest activity, such as shopping, may become a dreaded—and eventually an impossible—task.

The inevitably depressing effect of the panic syndrome may partly account for the greater than expected rate of suicide found in such patients (see Table 2-1).

A further disability associated with severe phobias of all kinds stems from the potential for self-medication with drugs or alcohol. Alcohol and the minor tranquilizers often prescribed by physicians frequently reduce the phobic's anxiety, but such artificial comfort may easily become habit-forming and lead to drug addiction or alcoholism.

Perhaps the best way to understand panic is to begin by exploring its nearest relatives, phobia and the common fears, in more detail. In this examination, two apparently opposing viewpoints will emerge. These are frequently summarized as "nature or nurture." On the one hand, there is evidence that a biological predisposition—perhaps, as we have seen, a multi-system disorder—underlies the development of the panic syndrome. On the other hand, it is also clear that learning is involved in the acquisition of the associated phobic behavior. The resolution of this conflict, and the implications of such a resolution for treatment, is a further aim of this book.

As the next chapter will explain, phobias are common and fears are widespread. This suggests that normal fears are, or have been, useful to survival. The tendency to avoid and to fear novel or potentially dangerous situations is obviously useful, and the ubiquitous nature of fears in childhood makes good sense: Children need to be protected from their ignorance of the world by an internal biological mechanism. Moreover, in earlier times, in a more physically dangerous world, fears and avoidance would have been even more useful. Why then should there be severe and obviously debilitating forms of anxiety, fear, and avoidance among adults today? Could it be that a protective mechanism has gone wrong?

FEARS ABOUND 3

Irrational fears have been described by poets, philosophers, and physicians through the ages. Shakespeare captures the phobic in these lines from *The Merchant of Venice*:

> Some men there are love not a gaping pig;
> Some, that are mad if they behold a cat.

One of the earliest descriptions of phobia comes from the Greek physician Hippocrates. He describes an unusual case: When Nicanor began to drink, the sound of the flute would disturb him; as soon as he heard the first note, terror would overcome him. Curiously, he could listen to the flute unmoved during the day; only when night fell, and perhaps when he started to drink, would the terror descend upon him. As this case illustrates, the circumstances that provoke fear can be quite specific.

Descartes and other philosophers, searching for the cause of these mysterious aversions, noted that many phobias begin early in life and proposed that maternal aversions might be transmitted to the embryo. This notion was incorporated into early medical writings. Thus the terror of King James I of England at the sight of an unsheathed sword was ascribed to his mother's having witnessed the assassination of a friend during her pregnancy. Today, we do not believe that fears or phobias can be acquired this way.

By the nineteenth century, physicians had begun to study phobias more systematically, attempting with an orgy of classification to make sense of the bewildering array of different aversions. Defined by names derived in the main from Greek roots, the most common fears took on a ponderous seriousness (see Table 3-1). Unfortunately, such a classificatory system does not guarantee precision in delineating phobias. It suggests, for example, that all agoraphobics have the same fears, when in reality the situations that provoke fear may be quite different for two people with apparently the same phobia.

One person with agoraphobia might fear being left alone at home and would need company all day long. Another might fear driving alone on freeways. The extent and type of phobic behavior is different in the two cases, yet both would be called agoraphobic. The first may share the fears of the second, but not vice versa. Some social phobics might fear large gatherings; the task of cocktail conversation proves so arduous that such persons gravitate to the edges of a party—if they can bring themselves to attend one. Others might fear authority figures and would have difficulty in expressing themselves to such persons in the course of their workday. Still others might fear any demonstration of anger. The fear could be equally severe in all these cases of social phobia; it is the fear-provoking circumstances that differ.

■

The difference between the common fear and the less common simple phobia is, as we have seen, one of degree. The common fear can be faced, though with discomfort, and causes little or no interference with everyday life. By contrast, a phobia is defined at least in part by the disability associated with it. Thus, a fear of heights might cause dizziness and anxiety in someone looking over the edge of a cliff or from the balcony of a tall building. Anyone with such a fear would stand back from the view, and that would be the extent of the avoidance. A height phobic, however, would avoid at almost any cost even being exposed to such situations, would not go into tall buildings—or would not venture higher than the first few floors—and would avoid trips that necessitate exposure to high places. In the case of the height *fear* there is little interference with the ordinary course of life; but in height *phobia*, considerable interference is evident. Even innocuous sounding phobias may be extremely disabling. Take, for example, the case of a young woman with a frog phobia—not a phobia one would suppose particularly troublesome. But this patient lived in Vermont, where small frogs abound during the spring and summer months. Housebound and unable to go to work for so large a part of the year, she had given up her career before being successfully treated.

TABLE 3-1

Some Common Fears and Phobias and Their Uncommon Names

Heights	*Acrophobia*
Open Spaces	*Agoraphobia*
Cats	*Ailourophobia*
Thunder	*Asterophobia*
Lightning	*Ceraunophobia*
Enclosed Spaces	*Claustrophobia*
Dogs	*Cynophobia*
Horses	*Equinophobia*
Dirt, Germs, Contamination	*Mysophobia*
Snakes	*Ophidiophobia*
Darkness	*Nyctophobia*
Running Water	*Potamophobia*
Fire	*Pyrophobia*
Stage Fright	*Topophobia*
Animals	*Zoophobia*

Phobia is, however, more than avoidance of a feared situation. The perception of a feared event sets off a chain of physiological and behavioral sequences. As Darwin observed,

> The frightened man at first stands like a statue, motionless or breathless, or crouches down as if instinctively to escape observation. The heart beats quickly and violently, so that it palpitates or knocks against the ribs.[4]

We are living in the bodies of our ancestors, bodies shaped by centuries of existence in a harsh environment quite different from that of modern times. The brisk response to a sudden noise or to a visual cue suggesting the form and movement of a reptile, while still useful today, was a necessity for survival in times past. The rapid response to such events— whether to freeze and crouch, thus halting exploration of a potentially dangerous situation and presenting the smallest possible target to a predator, or to leap like an athlete from the crouched position and flee the scene—is a complex integrated behavior undoubtedly shaped by its success in preserving life through countless generations. Even though we no longer live in such a physically dangerous world, these automatic reactions live on in our bodies. To move from the perception of danger to action requires but a fraction of a second, yet in that time nervous impulses have traveled from our senses (sight, hearing, touch, smell, taste) through the brain to alert a series of muscular and glandular responses that speed the heart, shunt blood from the gut to the muscles, tense those muscles to prepare for action, and supply them with oxygen by deepening our breathing.

The fear response as an instantaneous defensive reaction to danger has nursed mankind for thousands of years and is, I believe, virtually indistinguishable from the panic attack. We can think of the panic attack as set off by a faulty burglar alarm, forever signaling nonexistent danger. In the case of simple phobias (those without panic attacks) the same physiological and behavioral responses to the thought or actuality of the feared object or situation occur in muted form.

Most phobics manage to keep the fear response in check by avoiding the objects or situations that provoke anxiety. This is not always possible: A young woman was admitted to a hospital following an automobile accident in which her leg was broken when her car was crushed between two trucks on a narrow bridge. From the moment she regained consciousness following surgery, she was extraordinarily uncooperative with the nursing staff, often losing her temper with them. She reacted with alarm to the simplest medical procedures, was excessively demanding of attention, and disturbed other patients in the middle of the night with screams provoked by vivid nightmares. The nursing and medical staff thought that she might be suffering from a severe mental illness, perhaps a psychosis (a disorder in which the perception of reality is altered). In fact, she had awakened to find herself trapped in her phobic situation, a hospital.

As a very young child, this unfortunate young woman had suffered from a serious illness that had necessitated a long stay in bed, numerous painful injections and blood tests, and many physical examinations. During the course of this illness the association of doctors with pain and fear developed into a full-blown phobia. Since that time she had assiduously managed to avoid seeing a physician, even for routine checkups. Now, at twenty years of age, she was suddenly plunged into her most feared situation—a hospital—literally tied down to the bed, her broken leg suspended in the air. For her, this was analogous to someone with a fear of snakes falling into a snake pit; she was continually terrified. The only way to manage the situation—for even heavy sedation did not much help to diminish the anxiety—was to discharge her from the hospital and have her cared for at home. Again, avoidance behavior diminishes fear and anxiety, but has its cost.

■

Phobic avoidance may become even more disabling, for in the case of some phobias, particularly those involving a fear of injury either to the phobic or to someone else, a further elaboration may occur in the form of compulsive rituals. Such rituals take two main forms, checking and washing. In the case of checking, the compulsive fears that he may make a mistake that might hurt someone else; for example, switches on gas jets and electric ovens have to be checked over and over again to make sure that they are off, so that no harm will come to anyone. In the case of handwashing, the compulsive is avoiding the possibility of being infected or infecting others.

Take, for example, the person who develops a fear of infection. Like all phobics, he will avoid threatening situations, in this instance places where infection might occur; at first, for obvious reasons, hospitals, sickrooms, and sick people would be avoided. Avoidance might then spread to places where sick people might have been. Ultimately, most people and many places might be avoided because of the possibility of infection, a possibility that in the patient's view threatens a deadly illness.

Now a new turn of events occurs. The phobic becomes compulsive; he begins to wash his hands after being exposed—at least in his perception—to infection. Soon he realizes that he did not become sick and concludes that by continuing to wash his hands he can continue to escape contamination. Now a full-blown compulsive ritual may develop in which the patient washes his hands, often for hours at a time, to avoid being infected. His hands and arms may become excoriated, but his behavior is maintained by the simple observation that "as long as I wash my hands in this way I will not die." And if he should become sick, he will attribute the sickness to his failure to take sufficient precautions to avoid infection. The handwashing ritual is thus reinforced both by its "successes" and its "failures." There is no way out. Moreover, the performance of the compulsive rite takes up so much time and keeps him so isolated that the patient is no longer exposed to places or people associated with his primary fear of infection.

Such ritual avoidance may reach astounding proportions and may involve not only the sufferer but also the family members, who become inextricably entangled in the web of compulsive behavior. In our example, the phobic's home must become a place safe from disease. To assure him of this, the patient's parents may be required to engage in rituals of their own—for example, taking off their shoes when they enter the house and washing their hands thoroughly before touching anything, thus avoiding importing any contagious infection into the home. Soon they will have to wash everything that is brought home; even the groceries may have to be hosed off! Ultimately an almost aseptic technique will develop, with dirty clothing being carefully placed in plastic bags and being washed in a way that does not "contaminate." Ritual is piled upon ritual to avoid the fear, and the success of each addition in avoiding the central fear—death—reinforces the new behavior.

Obviously, in order to grow to such luxuriant proportions such behavior must be rooted in a fertile soil. The compulsive is often an exaggerated version of parents who are overconscientious in their own cleanliness. Once caught up in the compulsions there is no way out for the family, for any divergence from the elaborate routines leads to panic, often accompanied by temper tantrums on the part of the patient, so fiercely is the avoidance ritual defended. Thus the strict housekeeper is involuntarily converted into the zealot by her child.

■

Not only are phobias and their less frequent compulsive elaboration disabling, but they may also persist for a long time, although there is some controversy on this point. To investigate the duration of a phobia it is necessary to follow untreated cases for several years. Since clinicians treat their patients, subjects for such follow-up studies are rarely available. Some studies have suggested that the neuroses (anxiety-based disorders including mild depression), of which phobia is one, are relatively short-lived—a claim with which those clinicians who struggle over many years to help a patient disagree. On the other hand, clinicians probably see a biased sample of phobics, since only those with the more disabling phobias will seek help. Even long-term follow-up studies of treated phobics are relatively few. Those that have been undertaken report maintained recovery rates of between 20 and 40 percent from five to twenty years following treatment.

In a study bearing on this point, some colleagues and I surveyed a randomly chosen sample of phobics living in the small New England city of Burlington, Vermont, in the mid-1960s. We were able to identify phobic individuals, to assess the severity of their phobias, and to repeat this assessment five years later, paying particular attention to those who had not received treatment during this time. This was a perfect opportunity to examine the natural, untreated course of the condition.

Of the untreated phobics, including both adults and children, about 10 percent had become worse during the five-year period, and about 25 percent were unchanged. On the other hand, another 25 percent were now free of symptoms, and the remaining 40 percent had shown some improvement. This high rate of improvement, however, was mostly accounted for by the disappearance of phobias among the children and adolescents in the study. All of these had shown improvement, and fully 40 percent were free of symptoms. Thus age emerged as a major factor in predicting improvement: Children do well, adults do less well. When we extrapolate the degree of improvement achieved by the average adult beyond the five years of the study, we find that it would take about forty years to recover fully from a phobia without treatment. We must conclude that phobias are long-lasting, at least in adults.

It would seem reasonable to expect that the more severe the phobia, the longer the time required to recover from it. Surprisingly, this was not so. Severity of symptoms, as measured during the initial survey, did not affect outcome. Even relatively mild phobias persist. One factor did predict recovery or lack of it—the complexity of the phobia. Simple phobias, such as an isolated fear of heights or of animals, without panic attacks, tended to disappear more quickly than more complex phobias, such as agoraphobia, which, as we have seen, is often associated with other phobias, and always with panic attacks.

How frequent are phobias? The earliest data on the frequency of phobias came from a study of mental illness in the Yale–New Haven area conducted in the 1950s. In this study, only the number of cases of phobia actually receiving psychiatric treatment were counted. This method, of course, underestimates the rate of phobia in the community, as many people never seek treatment for such a condition, particularly if it is mild; and others may either have completed or not yet entered treatment at the time of the study. Nonetheless, phobia was found to account for 20 percent of all the neuroses being treated, and to exist at an estimated rate of one case for each two thousand of the general population.

Our study in Burlington allowed a finer look at the distribution of phobia in the general population, since all cases of phobia, whether

TABLE 3-2

Rate of Phobias in Burlington, VT, 1965
(in Descending Order)

General Population		In Treatment	
Type of Phobia	Frequency (in percentage)	Type of Phobia	Frequency (in percentage)
Illness/Injury	3.1%	Agoraphobia/Panic	50%
Storms	1.3	Illness/Injury	34
Animals	1.1	Death	4
Agoraphobia	0.6	Crowds	4
Death	0.5	Animals	4
Crowds	0.4	Heights	2
Heights	0.4	Darkness	2

or not they were receiving treatment, were counted. As shown in Table 3-2, in this study the number of phobics in the general population was far higher than one person per two thousand. Fully 7.5 percent of the population reported a mildly disabling phobia—one that interfered in some way with their lives. On the other hand, severe phobias—those that would lead to an inability to work, or would severely disrupt home and life—affected only two persons out of every thousand, and the most severely disabling disorder of all, compulsive ritualizing, was even less common, affecting fewer than one person in two thousand. Agoraphobia, an integral part of the panic syndrome, is by no means the most common phobia. Only six persons out of every thousand in the Burlington study reported having this disorder. Half of all phobics in treatment, however, suffered from agoraphobia.

Phobias and the panic syndrome, including both mild and severe cases, probably affect about 8 percent of the general population at some time during their lives. But common fears affect everyone. To better understand phobia and the panic syndrome, we first need to explore the normal fears and to wonder why we need to fear at all.

■

The ubiquitous distribution of the common fears piqued the interest of psychology from its earliest days. In 1897, G. Stanley Hall, writing in the *American Journal of Psychology*, a journal that he had founded just ten years earlier, began his article, "A Study of Fears," by questioning the method of introspection then widely used to collect data on psychological events. Some of his thoughts about the difficulties of psychological research have been repeated less eloquently by others over the ensuing years.

As psychological research has lately tended towards will and feeling, the limitations of both the experimental and the introspective methods have grown increasingly apparent, and in some directions are now exiguous and almost painful. We can neither excite the stronger emotions in the laboratory nor coolly study ourselves while they are on under natural conditions. . . . It was in view of this general situation that we have evoked the aid of the questionnaire method in this field. . . . By these means, too, psychology is brought into closer contact with human life over more and larger areas, and also given practical bearings.[5]

The method chosen by Hall to elicit information from volunteers about their fears is by modern standards inexact, since volunteers may not be representative of the general population. Similar criticisms were evoked decades later by the work of Kinsey, who studied an even touchier topic than fear, namely sexual behavior. Nonetheless, Hall's findings have held up over the years.

■

In Hall's study, 1,701 people described over six thousand fears, making for an average of nearly four fears each. The most detailed descriptions, he found, came from the one thousand boys and girls among his subjects. Their most common fears were of storms, snakes and other animals, darkness, strangers, fire, death, and disease.

Over the years, other workers have confirmed these findings. In the mid-1930s, Jersild and Holmes approached children with the following questions: "Tell me about things that scare you, things that frighten you. Tell me what makes you afraid. Tell me more about that. What else makes you afraid? What else scares you? What else? What else?"[6] Under this persistent questioning, children identified animals as the most frequently feared objects, followed by darkness, strangers, accidents, illness, and injuries. Relatively little had changed over the years.

Another study, in 1936, went further by actually exposing children to the unexpected sounds of a thunderstorm, which caused a fearful reaction in the great majority. This study led to the conclusion that the situations causing fear were characterized by a sudden strange sight or sound and that they often involved physical contact, but much less frequently actual pain.

The widespread nature of fears suggests that fears must have a function. An excellent case can be made for fear as a biological endowment aimed at protecting the young from potential dangers in the environment. As the child ventures farther away from the protection of its mother, so fear becomes the nursemaid, balancing the temptation of curiosity. Many studies that have examined fear and avoidance in animals support this hypothesis. Very young monkeys, for example, will approach almost any novel occurrence in the environment, and the larger, brighter, and more mobile the object of their attention, the more attracted they are. At about thirty days of age a remarkable change occurs: The very same events evoke fear and avoidance. From this we can deduce that the mother protects the infant monkey from its lack of discrimination during the first few weeks of life, but as its mobility and consequent physical separation from her increase, its own fearfulness emerges for its protection. Similar behavior is seen in the human infant: Smiling at any face, including those of strangers, begins at about eight weeks of age, but is replaced by a fear of strangers at six to eight months.

The fear of snakes, so common in humans, is almost universal in primates. Laboratory experiments with chimpanzees have revealed that rapid movement marked by sudden changes in direction is typical of fear-provoking events. Obviously a snake has just these characteristics. When snakes were carried into the monkey-house in the London zoo, all the monkeys fled, screaming. Only the lemurs—a species confined to Madagascar, where there are no snakes—showed curiosity rather than fear in the presence of these unexpected visitors.

It seems, then, that fear often holds curiosity in check. The blue jay, for instance, will approach a novel object with great caution. At first, it flies ever closer in order to observe it. Then it lands briefly and sidles closer and closer, until, ultimately, it will peck the object. If any rapid movement occurs, the bird flies away uttering warning cries. A similar oscillation between curiosity and caution bred of fear is seen in young children faced with a novel object or situation.

The protection afforded by this innate fear mechanism is useful even today, for the young would be exposed to more danger than they are were it not for the fear response. The fear of separation that binds the child to its mother is a protection that continues until the child is mature enough to avoid the more dangerous aspects of his or her world. As the child explores its environment, other fears protect against harm. The fear of heights, for example, will often dissuade

TABLE 3-3

Rate of Common Fears in Burlington, VT, 1965

Type of Fear	Percentage of Population	Percentage of Female Population	Percentage of Male Population
Snakes	30%	55%	20%
Heights	30	33	28
Storms	21	31	10
Flying	20	27	11
Dentists	20	22	17
Injury	18	18	19
Illness	17	20	12
Enclosed Spaces	12	14	10
Being Alone	12	16	8

the very young from attempting to climb trees; and if they do so, will, when they look down, tend to freeze them to the limb of the tree upon which they are precariously perched and will activate the cry for help as separation fear comes into play. All this protection is automatic. We truly have a guardian angel within ourselves.

■

Because the early studies of fear had, for the most part, focused on children, my colleagues and I examined the distribution of fears across all age groups as part of the Burlington study. We approached a randomly drawn sample of this small city and interviewed each member of those households selected separately. Mothers responded for children up to fourteen years of age.

No one was fearless. On the average, each person in the Burlington sample reported seven fears. This is higher than the number reported in most earlier studies, except for one study in the mid-1950s, which had also found the average number of fears to be seven—but in that instance among children. Are people becoming more fearful over time? Or are they becoming more honest about their fears? And is this perhaps in response to better methods of data collection? The latter explanation would seem the most likely.

As shown in Table 3-3, the findings in the Burlington study confirmed earlier studies; the most common fears were of snakes and small animals, of heights and storms, of doctors and dentists, of injury and illness, and of being alone. One new fear had been added— a fear of flying—which seemed to be a subcategory of the fear of injury.

When we sort out the basic elements of the various fears described in the Burlington study and in previous studies using statistical methods, three specific patterns emerge: fears of animals, of injury, and of separation. Each of the fears shown in Table 3-3 can be related to one or more of these categories. The fear of enclosures, for example, is related to being trapped and thus being exposed to injury, as well as being separated from others. It is tempting to speculate that the fear of animals still seen today is the pale remnant of a fear of predators, while injury fears are primarily directed toward physical dangers that might be encountered in the wild. Separation fear acts in concert with these other fear groupings by keeping the very young close by their mothers, thus protecting them from the dangerous environment. Should a child accidentally encounter one of these dangerous situations, the resulting scare would reinstate separation fear, restricting further exploration of the environment for a while.

Who suffers from these fears? In the Burlington study, 30 percent of the *total* population, but over half of the *female* population confessed to the most common fears. Females were more fearful than males in every category except that of injury. This excess of fears in females does not appear to be due to overreporting of fears by girls and women or underreporting by boys and men. Furthermore, experimental studies, in which children of both sexes and of the same age are exposed to fear-provoking situations, demonstrate that girls are more fearful than boys across the range of situations examined.

Why women should be more fearful than men is not entirely clear, but differences in social conditioning suggest a plausible explanation—that fearful responses in young children are treated differentially, according to the sex of the child. Direct observation of children's behavior during a medical examination showed that boys minimized their fear of pain, boasting that "It hurt, but I didn't cry . . . anybody that cries is a sissy." Girls, on the other hand, appealed for help to the nurse: "Let me sit on your lap" or "Let me hold your hand." Boys must not be sissies and must be brave in the face of fear. Girls, however, may seek help and protection. These differences in behavior are presumably learned, both by observation of others and by interaction with adults. Such differences undoubtedly affect the experience of fear and may even affect the number of fears and their severity.

On the other hand, it also makes biological sense for women, who are less physically able to defend themselves in the wild, and who will need extra protection while childbearing, to be endowed with a

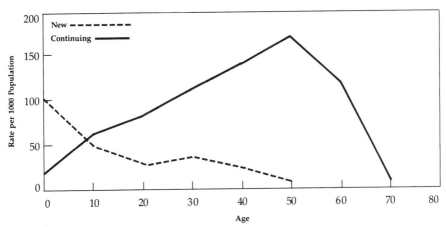

FIGURE 3-1
Rate of New and Continuing Fears in Burlington, VT, 1965

wider range of fears. This may be nature's way of ensuring the survival of humanity. Thus the propensity for women in our society to have more fears than men may have both biologic and social roots.

■

If specific fears are nature's way of providing protection from a potentially harmful environment, they should decline in frequency and in intensity as the need for protection diminishes with the approach of adulthood. Our study of fears in Burlington afforded an opportunity to examine this assumption, as persons of all ages were questioned. As shown in Figure 3-1 by the broken line, the rate of *new* fears declines during adolescence, and the decline continues into adult life.

That childhood fears tend to decline with maturity is confirmed in more detailed studies of children's fears. As usual, G. Stanley Hall was the first to make this observation. For both boys and girls, he found that the number of reported fears rose steadily until adolescence, when a decline set in. Hall also noted that in spite of the general decline of fearfulness, certain fears—such as the fear of snakes—tended to increase. In addition, social fears increase during adolescence.

These observations are consistent with the findings from the Burlington study. In that study, we were able to determine not only the number of *new* fears over time (shown by the broken line in Figure 3-1), but also the total number of fears (shown by the solid line). A short-lived fear is indicated when the solid line is very close to the broken line; wide separation of the two lines indicates that new fears are persisting for a long time. Thus, while a new fear of snakes seldom arises after mid-adolescence, the old fears persist throughout life. This pattern also holds for fears of animals, heights, enclosures, and storms. On the other hand, fears of injections, doctors, and strangers disappear somewhat more quickly. These patterns make some sense, since those in the first category seem to pose a physical danger even to adults, and their persistence into adult life would thus be beneficial while those in the second category threaten little harm to the adult.

The life cycle of fears has also been studied in the laboratory. When children of different ages are presented with feared objects and introduced into feared situations, the results, although gathered over a shorter time span, are consistent with the questionnaire findings. All the fears tested in this more objective way declined from the age of two years to six years, with the exception of fears of snakes and dogs, which remained high.

That curiosity and the resulting confrontation with previously feared situations get the better of most fears is apparent. Those fears persisting into adult life would seem to persist because they have a protective value; yet we know that in some individuals fears with no demonstrable value or use persist. Do the common fears form the basis for the more severe problems that we label phobias? To answer this question, we need to examine the relationship between fears and phobias more closely.

■

One reason to suspect a relationship between fears and phobias is that the Burlington study revealed a continuum between the more severe common fears and the less severe phobias. The line dividing fear and phobia is drawn somewhat arbitrarily and the distinction rests mainly, as we have seen, upon the degree of disability associated with the problem.

There are, however, even stronger reasons to suspect a relationship. Earlier in this chapter we saw that it was possible to sort out the main patterns of fear from the complex mass of fears reported by individuals. Exactly the same approach can be taken to the symptoms reported by phobics. When this is done, the similarities to the findings with common fears are striking.

Two dominant themes emerge. One is the class of injury phobias, of which animal phobias appear to be a special and somewhat separate case; the other is the class of phobias based upon separation. These are the same groupings found in the case of fears, strongly suggesting that the origins of phobias are to be found in the persistence of the common fears of childhood into adulthood.

Further evidence that childhood fears may turn into phobias appears when we examine the ages at which different kinds of phobias begin. Animal and injury phobias begin in childhood, at an average age of four. On the other hand, agoraphobia, a component of the panic syndrome, begins in adult life at an average age of twenty-four. Bearing in mind the distinction between injury fears and separation fears, and remembering that a separation often precedes the onset of the panic syndrome, it is tempting to speculate that the panic syndrome forms a class of phobias deriving from an accentuated childhood separation fear, precipitated by a separation experience in adult life.

■

What, then, are separation fears? And is there a clinical syndrome, similar to animal and injury phobias, that occurs in childhood? Most children become upset at one time or another when their parents leave, even if the separation is brief and the child is left with someone he or she knows. This is normal separation fear, which protects the young from hurt by keeping them close to their mothers. The same fear is apparent in the shy clinging of a child to its mother on the first day of nursery school. Much more serious is a full-blown school phobia, in which the child adamantly refuses to attend school.

When school phobia was first recognized and separated from truancy about fifty years ago, it was thought that the affected child must be avoiding something at school, perhaps a punitive teacher or the school bully; hence the term "school phobia"—a fear or avoidance of school—was inaugurated. But this view did not turn out to be true; hardly ever is anything wrong at school. The disorder usually appears in a child attending elementary school. He or she complains of a headache or a stomachache on Sunday evening or Monday morning, without any evidence of illness. Once the decision is made to allow the child to stay home, the symptoms miraculously disappear. If the parent insists and tries to take the child to school, there are tears, the child clings desperately to the parent, develops symptoms in school, and may even run home at the first opportunity.

The true nature of this problem was forcefully demonstrated to me by an experience with one of my patients many years ago. This seven-year-old school-phobic boy was brought to see me by his mother. After interviewing the two of them together, I wanted to talk to the child alone, so I asked his mother to leave the room. This she did, taking her son by the hand and walking out. I suggested that she leave alone, and I took hold of her son's other hand, in what became, for a moment, a tug-of-war. As soon as the door was closed behind his mother, the little boy panicked, rushed around the office knocking things awry, and out of the door. Evidently the problem presented by the school phobic is not a fear of school, but a fear of separation from mother. Moreover, this mother also showed a distinct difficulty in separating from her son.

The symptoms of the school-phobic child are surprisingly similar to those of an adult agoraphobic. First, there is the phobic limitation; the child will not go anywhere without his or her mother or father. Similarly, the adult agoraphobic needs a companion in order to leave home comfortably. Second, there is the hypochondriacal preoccupation with physical symptoms, often accompanied by fear that some dread illness will strike. This, as we have seen, is a feature of the panic syndrome. Third, there is panic precipitated by separation.

A more subtle expression of separation fear is seen in the preoccupation of the school-phobic child with ideas of the death or illness of the parent. The child may say that he does not want to leave home "in case something happens," or he may feel impelled to check on the well-being of one or both parents. Such thoughts, either of his own illness or death or that of a parent, symbolize the threat of separation. They are also tinged with feelings of sadness and depression. Again, these thoughts and the feeling of depression are similar to the symptoms experienced by the victim of the panic syndrome. The question now becomes, Do those with the panic syndrome more frequently have a history of school phobia than a control group of persons with other phobias?

Interestingly, there have been very few studies of the early history of agoraphobics that bear on this issue. In the best such study, the histories of school phobia in sixty-six agoraphobics and simple phobics were compared: 44 percent of the agoraphobics reported such symptoms and only 24 percent of the simple phobics—a statistically significant difference. Separation anxiety may well underlie phobia in a substantial proportion of agoraphobics.

There are two reasons why fears and phobias might be found more frequently in some families than others: First is the influence of heredity, and second, that of learning. Separating the effects is extraordinarily difficult. Do fears and phobias even tend to run in families? To conduct a distortion-free survey is difficult. For example, simply asking persons with phobias about the psychiatric symptoms of family members might, because of the patient's own problem, lead to an excessive recollection of phobic symptoms in relatives.

The research method of taking a family history now consists of directly interviewing as many first-degree relatives (parents and siblings) as possible, using a standard interview technique. Diagnostic categories are then assigned from the interview records by another member of the research team who does not know which relative is which. Agreement between diagnoses can be determined by having two researchers assign diagnoses for a subsample of cases. This helps to overcome the bias of an interviewer who is interested in proving a particular hypothesis. While a substantial advance over the less rigorous methods used in the past, even this method cannot distinguish between the contribution of learning and that of inheritance. To make this distinction it is necessary to study the rate of occurrence of a given condition in identical and nonidentical twins. If heredity is a factor, then the rate in identical twins should exceed that of nonidentical twins.

The purist can still argue that learning might confound these results. Identical twins might be treated more similarly than nonidentical twins, which in turn might affect their learning of particular behavior patterns. To overcome this objection, adoptive studies must be carried out. Here the comparison is between the rate of the disorder in adopted children and in natural children of parents having the disorder. Adopted children presumably experience a different learning environment from that provided by natural parents suffering from the disorder, thus controlling for the effects of learning.

Fears have long been thought to run in families. Studies in the 1930s found that fearful mothers tend to have fearful children. In addition, children shared the same kinds of fears as their mothers. Our Burlington study showed similar results. Highly fearful children tended to come from those families with more fearful parents, a finding particularly true for mothers and daughters. And again, similar types

TABLE 3-4

Phobia in the Family

Relatives of Phobics		Relatives of Nonphobic Controls	
Relationship	Percentage with Phobia	Relationship	Percentage with Phobia
Fathers	4.2%	Fathers	1.2%
Mothers	30.6	Mothers	2.3
Brothers	6.0	Brothers	2.0
Sisters	10.0	Sisters	2.0

of fears were shared by parent and child. Of the eleven most common fears, seven were found to be shared, that is, to occur beyond the levels expected if chance alone were to determine the way in which fears were distributed. There is, however, one problem that may color the results of studies of the distribution of fears in families, namely that mothers answer the fear questionnaire for their children and may be more likely to report for their children fears similar to their own. Against this is the finding that children, if interviewed directly, report many more fears than their mothers report about them.

More definitive work has been done with the family patterning of phobias than of fears. As can be seen in Table 3-4, where data from the two early studies have been combined, the evidence suggests that phobia is more likely to be reported in the relatives of phobics than in the relatives of nonphobics. Particularly striking are the relatively large percentages of mothers and sisters of phobic patients who have a phobia, as compared with the controls.

More recently a large family study was conducted, in which the children of persons diagnosed as having depression with and without agoraphobia were directly interviewed. While this study concentrated on a somewhat atypical sample of agoraphobics, the results were interesting. Children of persons suffering only from depression were found to have no agoraphobia or school phobia. On the other hand, 16.7 percent of the children of persons diagnosed as having both depression and agoraphobia were found to have either agoraphobia or school phobia. Equally interesting, children of parents suffering both depression and agoraphobia had twice the risk of experiencing a major depression as children of parents with only depression (22 percent versus 10.5 percent).

There is, then, reasonable evidence that the agoraphobia-panic syndrome runs in families. In addition, we have repeatedly seen depression and agoraphobia related in some way. Our studies, however, cannot yet distinguish the mechanism responsible for the familial association. Is the disorder spread by inheritance or transmitted by learning? As noted earlier, to answer this question, a twin study is needed. Only one exists, a study of twenty-one pairs of twins in which one of each pair had been admitted to a hospital and had been diagnosed as having phobia. In the case of identical twins, 88 percent of the nonhospitalized twins were diagnosed as having phobia. For nonidentical twins only 38 percent received such a diagnosis. These data argue strongly that inheritance plays at least some part in the transmission of the more severe phobias. However, as we saw earlier, to be quite sure of this conclusion, data from an adoption study are needed. No such study presently exists.

■

It seems likely that separation fear, an inherited protective mechanism guarding the child from the vicissitudes of early life, instead of disappearing as it normally should, persists in some individuals, leading to school phobia during childhood, and to the panic syndrome in adult life. Possible reasons for such persistence include both faulty learning and faulty biological processes. On the biological side, we have seen that it is likely that inheritance plays an important role in the transmission of phobias. Depression and the panic syndrome may be linked genetically. It is also possible that chemical processes occurring very early in development may produce tissue alterations characteristic of some persons with the panic syndrome. On the other hand, it seems likely that fear-enhancing life experiences might deepen and prolong normal separation fear.

The influences of biology and learning are often posed as contrasting explanations for a given disorder. One of them will provide the correct answer from which will flow the definitive treatment. Although we will examine these two influences separately in the next two chapters, we will find that learning and biology can be viewed as short- and long-term transmission mechanisms, and that, surprisingly, the two merge in the chemical processes taking place within the brain cell. And just as learning and biology interact in the causation of this disorder, so do they in its treatment, where the combination of drugs and learning-based treatments seems to be better than either treatment alone.

LEARNING TO AVOID 4

A t the turn of the century, Freud, the founder of psychoanalysis, proposed that phobias are shaped by hidden conflicts, that they are not what they seem to be, and that their true nature can be discovered only by uncovering those hidden conflicts.

■

In 1909, Freud published a case history entitled "The Analysis of a Phobia in a Five-Year-Old Boy,"[7] commonly referred to as the case of "Little Hans." Early in January 1908, Hans, then five years old, developed a fear of horses. His symptoms were a dread of going out in the streets—apparently caused by a fear that a horse might bite him—and an accompanying fear of horse-drawn vehicles, together with depression in the evenings. These symptoms started after Hans witnessed an accident in which a horse harnessed to a bus fell to the ground. It should be noted that a fear of horses is not particularly unusual, although fear of a dog would be more common today.

Freud conducted the analysis of this case largely by mail, depending for information upon letters written by the boy's father, who was an enthusiastic adherent of Freud's theories. Freud saw the child only once. Thus the data for this crucial case, on which the early psychoanalytic theory of phobia was based, are secondhand observations, perhaps biased by Freud's pre-existing theories.

Among the critical events reported to have preceded the outbreak of the phobia was a rather lively interest in the facts of life. When Hans was three years of age, the following conversation reportedly took place while he was watching his mother undress.

Mother: "What are you staring like that for?"
Hans: "I was only looking to see if you'd got a widdler too."
Mother: "Of course. Didn't you know that?"
Hans: "No, I thought you were so big you'd have a widdler like a horse."

A few months later another incident took place, which Freud interpreted as an attempt to seduce his mother. She was drying him and powdering him after a bath, and at the same time attempting not to touch his penis.

Hans: "Why don't you put your finger there?"
Mother: "Because that would be piggish."
Hans: "What's that? Piggish? Why?"
Mother: "Because it's not proper."
Hans: (laughing) "But it's great fun."

On the day the phobia began, Hans went for a walk to the park with his nursemaid. During the walk, he started to cry and said that he wanted to "coax" (caress) his mother. This behavior, combined with the earlier reports of little Hans's budding sexual interest, led Freud to his first interpretation of the phobia: Namely, that Hans was very fond of his mother and wanted to be taken into her bed and that the reason he was afraid of horses was because of the interest he had taken in their "widdlers," and that these two facts were closely connected.

As a result of Freud's advice, a long series of conversations between Hans and his father began, in which various sexual longings were discussed. These conversations, duly reported in 140 pages, led to the basic interpretation of the phobia, namely that little Hans wanted to have his mother to himself but was afraid that his father would retaliate. Thus, he displaced his fear of being injured (castrated?) by his father onto the horse, which, like his father, had a big widdler, and which threatened to bite him. A big fear hid behind a little fear! Moreover, by avoiding horses and staying at home, he gained more attention from his mother, thus achieving one of his aims. Such economy is, in Freud's view, one of the hallmarks of neurosis.

This interpretation was confirmed in the following conversation, in which little Hans found an ingenious solution to his dilemma while playing a game with his imaginary children.

Father: "Hullo, are your children still alive? You know quite well that a boy can't have any children."

Hans: "I know. I was their Mummy before, now I'm their Daddy."

Father: "And who's the children's Mummy?"

Hans: "Why, Mummy, and you're their Granddaddy."

Father: "So then you'd like to be as big as me, and be married to Mummy, and then you'd like her to have children."

Hans: "Yes, that's what I'd like, and then my [paternal] Grandmamma will be their Grannie."

A neat solution! No one is harmed, and father is promoted to grandfather. At about this time, the phobia was resolved and it was Freud's view that its disappearance was connected to the solution of the Oedipus conflict.

Freud's theory emphasized that the various misconceptions of little Hans led to anxiety and that this anxiety was projected onto the horse, causing the phobia. One of the problems with this kind of case report, as critics have pointed out, is that any number of other interpretations are possible, and there is no way to be sure which is correct. Moreover, the conversations during which various interpretations of the problem are made influence future behavior, perhaps giving rise to a self-fulfilling prophecy. Indeed a very simple explanation of Hans's phobia has been put forward, namely that it was the sight and sounds of the accident that caused the phobia. Hans himself agreed with this interpretation: "When the horse in the bus fell down, it gave me such a fright really. That was when I got the nonsense [phobia]." Can the pairing of a loud noise with a previously unfeared object, the horse in this case, lead to a phobia? Interestingly, another little boy featured in the investigation of this possibility.

■

Ten years after the publication of the case of little Hans, a more experimentally oriented account of the origins of a phobia was presented by John B. Watson, entitled "Conditioned Emotional Reactions." This study was based on Pavlov's discovery of the conditioned reflex, in which learning could occur by the temporal association of two events. Using the principle of conditioning, Watson attempted to produce a phobia in an infant.

The subject of his experiment was an eleven-month-old baby, Albert B., whose mother was a wet nurse in a home for invalid children;

thus Albert had been raised from birth in a hospital environment. Not only was he brawny, weighing twenty-one pounds at nine months, but he rarely cried or showed fear. This emotional stability was confirmed in the laboratory by presenting Albert with various stimuli— a white rat, a rabbit, a dog, a monkey, masks with and without hair, cotton wool, burning newspapers, and so on. All these objects left Albert unmoved. His only response was to reach out and touch most of them. Only a loud noise induced crying.

To induce a phobia in such a paragon of mental health is a touchy business. As Watson reports,

> At first there was considerable hesitation upon our part in making the attempt to set up fear reactions experimentally. A certain responsibility attaches to such a procedure. We decided finally to make the attempt, comforting ourselves by the reflection that such attachments would arise anyway as soon as the child left the sheltered environment of the nursery for the rough and tumble of the home.[8]

So, when Albert was eleven months and three days old, Watson once more checked to see that he was without fear of the various stimuli and then began the experiment.

The method used to condition the fear was very simple. A white rat was placed in front of Albert, and when he reached for it, a loud noise was made by striking a hammer on a steel bar suspended behind him. The reaction was as might be expected. As Watson notes, on the second pairing, "just as the right hand touched the rat, the bar was again struck. Again, the infant jumped violently, fell forward and began to whimper. After two trials the experiment was suspended for a week, so as not to upset Albert too much."

A week later, after five more pairings of noise and the rat, Albert had developed a phobia. "The instant the rat was shown the baby began to cry. Almost instantly he turned sharply to the left, fell over on his left side, raised himself on all fours, and began to crawl away so rapidly that he was caught with difficulty before reaching the edge of the table." Moreover, Albert now showed a more generalized fear of stimuli associated with or similar to the rat, such as rabbits, dogs, cotton wool, and sealskin, fears that had not been present before the conditioning experiment. But he continued unafraid of objects unlike those associated with the loud noise.

Unfortunately, the experiment ended there, for Albert left the hospital for home, taking the newly acquired phobia with him. As Watson notes in his epilogue, "The Freudians twenty years from now, unless their hypotheses change, when they come to analyze Albert's fear of a sealskin coat—assuming that he comes to analysis at that age—will probably tease from him the recital of a dream which, upon their analysis, will show that Albert at three years of age attempted to play with the pubic hair of the mother and was scolded violently for it." As even Watson admitted, such an event might very well condition a phobia, but in the case of little Albert the interpretation would have been incorrect.

Watson's production of an experimental phobia that looked very much like the real thing suggested that phobias could be learned by association of a neutral event with one that is alarming. It did not, however, answer the question: Are phobias caused in this way in the real world? Such a question is not easy to answer since it depends in part upon the memory of phobics concerning the events involved in the genesis of their problem.

■

Some case reports of adult phobics confirm Watson's findings that phobias can be learned by association. The most interesting of these were described by Bagby in 1922. His first case was that of a young woman who had retained since childhood a severe fear of running water but who could not remember any precipitating incident for the fear. She recalled that as a child she had a severe fear reaction to any sound of running water, and it often required three members of her family to hold her down while she was being bathed. As a child, when she traveled by train, it was necessary to keep the window covered, lest she see a stream.

During her twentieth year, a dramatic event occurred. An aunt, whom she had not seen for thirteen years, visited. Her first words to her niece were, "I have never told." These words provoked her recall of the original cause of the phobia: As a little girl of seven she had gone on a picnic with her mother and aunt. After lunch her mother had gone home, but she had asked to stay on. Later on, while she and her aunt were walking in the woods, the little girl, temporarily disobedient, had run off by herself. After a search, her aunt found her screaming in terror; she was wedged between two rocks, with a waterfall noisily pouring over her head. She begged her aunt not to tell her mother of her disobedience, and her aunt agreed. She returned home phobic. Here we have a perfect example of the pairing of a hitherto neutral and common substance—water—with a terrifying situation, leading after only one traumatic experience to a profound phobia. Yet the original incident was forgotten, and the aunt never told her story!

Bagby's second case is equally interesting, involving a middle-aged man who had a phobic fear of being grasped from behind. This fear prevented him from frequenting crowded places. In social situations, he would sit with his back to the wall. He could recall no precipitating circumstance, although the fear had persisted since childhood. The explanation was revealed during a visit to the town in which he was reared. Now fifty-five years old, he found an old friend still serving behind the counter of the neighborhood grocery. During a series of reminiscences the grocer remarked, "I want to tell you something that occurred when you were a boy. You used to go by this store on errands, and when you passed, you often took a handful of peanuts from the stand in front. One day just as you put your hand in the pile of peanuts, I jumped out and grabbed you from behind. You screamed and fell fainting to the sidewalk." Here again, one traumatic experience led to a long-lasting and severe phobia.

These cases are reminiscent of one of my own patients, a middle-aged woman suffering from claustrophobia who was able to recall the childhood incident upon which her fear was based. The phobia was so severe that she slept—and this was in the northern part of New York—with the door and every window removed from her bedroom. She was able to drive her car only if every window was open and if she could hold open the car door with one hand. The precipitating incident had occurred when she was playing with some neighborhood friends in a shop belonging to the father of one of her friends. The father was an undertaker, and the shop was full of coffins. On a dare, she got into one of the coffins, and her friends immediately sat on the lid, ignoring her terrified screams. She emerged a claustrophobic. Again, one dreadful experience led to a long-lasting and severe phobia.

■

Although these and similar cases provide evidence that phobias can be acquired through the simple pairing of an alarming occurrence and a hitherto neutral situation, the sad fact remains that such stories are rare. Few phobics can recall the precipitating incident for their fear.

Furthermore, evidence from other sources raises problems that this theory, which claims that a phobia is learned by association, cannot resolve.

While ethical considerations now bar experiments such as that conducted by Watson, war presents us with the conditions for a large-scale experiment when great numbers of civilians are exposed to bombing attacks. In such attacks, loud noise is paired with a variety of hitherto neutral events. According to the theory of learning by association, this type of conditioning should generate a large number of phobias. Yet surveys of exposed populations do not support this view. One survey of 8,000 schoolchildren exposed to bombing attacks in Bristol found that only 4 percent of the children developed anxiety symptoms attributable to air raids. The vast majority of children, 96 percent, were unaffected. Studies in Germany and Japan produce similar findings. Air raids caused acute emotional reactions such as irritability, a startled reaction to loud noise, and disturbed sleep in many people; but in the vast majority of cases, these symptoms vanished in a few days, and no permanent effects occurred. This, then, is a failure of the conditioning theory of phobia on a gigantic scale. Although, as we have seen, such experiences can generate a phobia, in most cases they do not.

Laboratory studies also cast doubt upon the conditioning theory of phobia. Fears conditioned by association tend to be short-lived. Most conditioned reflexes will weaken and disappear after a few exposures to the fear-provoking event, quite unlike the more persistent fear and avoidance behavior that we call a phobia. One important finding may, however, help to resolve this problem and explain how a conditioned fear response could persist and become a phobia. Avoidance of a feared situation blocks the normal process of unlearning the fear response.

Fear and avoidance behavior can be produced in animals by first exposing them to a signal followed by an electric shock, and then, following the onset of the signal, letting them press a lever to avoid the shock. Under these circumstances avoidance behavior becomes long-lasting. Here we have a situation very similar to a phobia, in which any sign indicating that a phobic situation is near leads to immediate avoidance. In the case of air raids, which are unavoidable for a civilian, we would expect the fear response to be transient. *Only if the phobic situation is avoidable, as it usually is, would we expect the phobia to be long-lasting.*

■

Attempts to replicate Watson's production of a phobia in children have not always been successful. There are some objects that cannot be associated with fear. The pairing of a loud noise with geometrically shaped objects, for example, does not lead to a phobia. Only some objects can become feared. If all objects were equally capable of becoming associated with fear, then fears should be distributed randomly across all objects in the environment, but surveys of fears in large populations show that this is not so. As we have seen, all surveys show that only certain classes of objects arouse fear; fears of animals, heights, and storms occur with comparable frequency in all the surveys.

Some recent experiments provide more detail about fear responses to different types of objects. While the experimental production of full-blown phobias in humans is not ethically defensible, mini-phobias that are detectable by means of sophisticated physiological recording devices can be produced without risk of a disabling illness. In such experiments mild electric shocks are paired with an object, and the experimenter then examines the physiological responses—of which the subject is usually unaware—by using a recorder that amplifies small reactions. The reactions usually measured are the electrical resistance of the skin and the amount of blood flowing through a finger, both of which change with anxiety.

The results are not surprising. Once more it is clear that it is easier to associate a fear response with objects such as snakes or spiders—usually presented in pictorial form—than with objects such as flowers, or geometrical shapes or designs. (Rapid conditioning occurs with snakes, and one trial often produces long-lasting mini-phobias.) Moreover, the perceived unpleasantness of the object increases following conditioning, but again this is true only for objects such as snakes and spiders. More complex stimulus patterns have also been found to lead to the formation of mini-phobias—for example, presenting the subject with two versions of the same object. Thus, it is possible to condition a phobia to an angry face but not to a smiling face. (One can hypothesize that this kind of fear-learning might be useful in helping the young avoid angry elders, thus preventing social rebuff, or even injury.) Conditioning to man-made dangerous objects such as guns does not occur. Could this be because such weapons were not present early in our evolutionary history?

Just as people tend to develop phobias only to certain types of *objects*, they tend to respond to phobia-conditioning only when certain types of *fear-evoking stimuli* are coupled with these objects. The observations from the mini-phobia experiments provide the evidence here. Even with snakes and spiders, only stimuli such as electric shocks produce the mini-phobia. Loud noise does *not* produce a fear response to such animals. This result suggests that *only certain sensory pathways* are involved in the acquisition of this type of fear response. Could it be because snakes and spiders bite that tactile stimuli produce the fear?

The results of the experiments with mini-phobias combine with the epidemiological evidence to strengthen the hypothesis that we examined earlier—that humans are primed to produce fear responses only to certain classes of dangerous situations, such as animals, heights, or separation. The association of such objects or situations with fear arousal leads to very rapid fear-learning, which then persists if the feared situations are avoided.

■

Let us now pursue another line of inquiry and examine the assumption that some phobias may be learned by social transmission without the primary experience of arousal in the presence of the feared object. Such transmission may be either by imitation or direct communication.

Almost all the experimental evidence that fear can be transmitted socially derives from recent animal work. In the most compelling experiment, young monkeys—who had been raised in the laboratory and who therefore had no fear of snakes—were allowed to observe their parents, who had been raised in the wild, react fearfully to toy and real snakes. After only eight minutes, the young monkeys had developed a strong fear of snakes. After six sessions, the young monkeys' fear was indistinguishable from that of their parents. Moreover, the more disturbed their parents had been by the snakes, the greater the fear in the offspring.

In a later experiment, another group of young monkeys watched adult monkeys who were strangers to them. Again a fear of snakes developed, but this time the fear was less strong and showed greater variation than that of the monkeys who learned by observing their fearful parents. It seems clear that social learning can give rise to phobic-like behavior, and that parents are the best fear transmitters! We would expect such learning to be particularly strong in humans, since fears might be transmitted by verbal or nonverbal communication.

While there is no direct experimental evidence for such transmission in humans, case studies do provide some confirmation for this hypothesis, particularly in the case of school phobia, which, as we have seen, may be regarded as separation anxiety. An actual description of a mother leaving her school-phobic twins is instructive. She "bade her twins goodbye, with many reassurances of an early return. They played on unconcerned. She stopped again at the door to assure them they had nothing to fear. They glanced up but played on. Having gotten her coat, she made a third curtain speech in a tremulous voice, 'Don't be afraid. Mommy will be back. Please don't cry.' This time one of the twins got the cue and cried wildly."[9]

As one mother of an adolescent phobic patient noted, "I realize that I overreact to my daughter's going out by herself, just as I did when she was a child; now I try and keep my fears to myself." Another mother described her method of communicating fears to her daughter: "I am always doing things for her that she could easily do for herself. I seem to be afraid that she cannot do them. I often stop her from doing things by telling her to be careful or by doing them for her." Clearly, it is possible for the overanxious parent to subtly communicate fearfulness, thus stopping the normal exploration of the environment and the development of adequate means of coping with fears.

■

So far we have considered only feared events that occur outside the individual. But thoughts and memories may evoke almost as much fear as an event in the real world. Memories seem to be laid down in clusters. The more frequently two events are associated, the more likely it is that remembering one event will call to mind the other. Moreover, action tendencies, such as avoidance, are also set into motion by remembrances.

It seems likely that a relatively simple fear or phobia, for example a fear of snakes, is represented in memory with relatively few connections. The circumstances that will set off the fear and avoidance behavior are limited. On the other hand, a complex fear, such as that seen in the panic syndrome, is represented by many connections, so that a single aspect of the phobic stimulus will then arouse many thoughts and feelings. In the case of the panic syndrome, merely entering a crowded shopping center may evoke a feeling of claustrophobia. This may in turn call forth memories of previous panic attacks in such situations, or feelings of helplessness; and as such memories alter physiological arousal, the bodily sensations evoked may call to mind fears of illness, of losing control, and so on. These thoughts, in turn, arouse further fear. Memory acts as a magnifier of fear. A vivid imagination may not be helpful to the phobic.

■

All of these observations lead to a clearer understanding of the various ways in which fears might be learned. Certain classes of visual and auditory events activate a biologically endowed learning mechanism. Such events form two clusters: (1) those events, often sudden in onset, that portend possible injury, including social injury, and (2) happenings that threaten separation. Fear of these threatening situations is quickly learned and avoidance persists as a means of protecting the individual from a potentially harmful environment. Such learning can occur in several ways, but it seems likely that social transmission of fear, by alarm or by observation of a frightened parent, may be the main method. Other methods, such as the pairing of a traumatic event with a previously neutral situation, similar to the little Albert experiment, also occur, although their frequency may be less than might have been anticipated from early theories about fear.

This summary picture accounts only for the initial learning and persistence of fear, however, and not for that prolongation that we call phobia. It seems likely that repeated expressions of alarm by a fearful parent might reinforce avoidance of the feared situation. Moreover, fearful parents may also actively prevent their children from exploring the environment, thus depriving them of the opportunity to extinguish their fears by experience. Finally, as we have seen in the previous chapter, some individuals may be born with a predisposition to learn avoidance behavior more quickly and more persistently than others. This possibility, together with an exploration of the processes accompanying fear or arousal in the brain, form the themes of the next chapter.

A PHOBIC 5
PREDISPOSITION

Although our behavior is regulated by our interaction with the outside world, complex and still mysterious processes within the brain modulate what we do, think, and feel. These processes, often taking place in ultra-microscopic structures, are less accessible to study than is behavior, which can be directly observed. Often to study them means to destroy, since actual brain tissue may be needed for chemical analysis. Much of the work, therefore, must be carried out in animals. It is, of course, not at all clear that animals experience complex feeling states such as anxiety or depression. Remarkable progress has nevertheless been made in understanding not only how the brain works, but how the functioning of the brain relates to specific disorders such as anxiety.

We know that some individuals consistently react intensely and in a more persistent fashion to situations that others find not at all troubling or only a little bothersome. This suggests the existence within the central nervous system of a control system that modulates behavior; it can be thought of as roughly comparable to the control mechanism on a television set that determines whether the picture is too bright or too dark and makes the necessary adjustment. The setting of the human mechanism would determine the degree of fearfulness exhibited by any particular individual. Another characteristic of this control system should be that experience could alter its setting, since as we have seen, learning is implicated in fear, phobia, and panic.

■

The brain cells, called neurons, and their complex interconnections are the infrastructure of our experience. A neuron looks rather like a starfish with a long string, or *axon*, attached to one end. Each axon ends in a nerve terminal, which lies close to one *dendrite*, or tentacle, of another neuron. The space between the two is the *synaptic cleft*.

It has long been known that electrical impulses pass from cell bodies down the axon to other cells via the dendrites. The mechanism for this transmission is exquisitely delicate. Cells are bathed in a sea of chemicals, the most important of which, from the viewpoint of electrical transmission, are sodium and potassium. Variations in the concentration of these chemicals inside and outside the cell determine the electrical potential across the cell membrane. Small channels allow them to flow into or out of the cell, changing the electrical potential, and allowing a current to flow along the cell surface. These chemical/electrical changes underlie the cells' ability to communicate with each other.

Electrical impulses, however, are not solely responsible for the interplay between nerve cells. Rather, they promote the synthesis and release of other chemicals known as *neurotransmitters* into the synaptic cleft. These neurotransmitters carry more precise messages. One of the critical experiments demonstrating the existence of such transmitter substances was carried out in the 1920s. A frog's heart was removed from its body and perfused with saline. When the vagus nerve, leading to the heart, was stimulated, the heart slowed down. When the saline circulating through this heart was allowed to flow through a second isolated heart, the second heart also slowed down. This indicated that a substance must have been released by stimulating the nerve of the first heart. The substance was eventually found to be *acetylcholine*, already known to be an inhibitory chemical. In the past quarter-century, similar transmitter substances have been found within the brain.

Within the neuron, in the cell body, protein building blocks are used to synthesize specific neurotransmitters. These chemicals are stored in vesicles until they are needed. Electrical impulses impinging upon the dendrites of a neuron from a variety of sources eventually lead to a change. Calcium flows into the cell and, upon reaching a critical concentration, causes the vesicles containing a neurotransmitter to migrate to the cell surface, where they fuse to the membrane and spill their contents into the synaptic cleft. Molecules of the neurotransmitter then diffuse rapidly across the narrow space toward the ending of another neuron. Here a fascinating structure, a *receptor site* specifically attuned to a particular transmitter, is waiting.

FIGURE 5-1
An Outline of Signal Transmission within the Brain

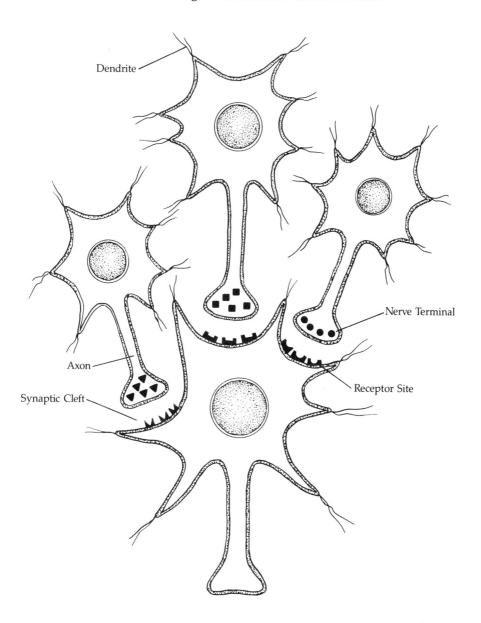

The neurotransmitter behaves very much like a space capsule docking at a satellite. Each molecule of the neurotransmitter whirls through the small space of the synaptic cleft toward its receptor site. Only a particular molecular shape will fit a receptor site. Thus, specificity of action is preserved. Once the neurotransmitter molecule is locked onto the receptor, changes in the degree of membrane permeability to potassium or to sodium occur, with a resulting electrical impulse. So electrical impulses are transformed to chemical messengers, and back again to electrical impulses, as messages flow from cell· to cell.

Regulation of these messages, and ultimately the regulation of behavior, can occur in several ways. First, excess molecules of neurotransmitter are rapidly mopped up by enzymes that deactivate them. An oversupply of such an enzyme could thus alter the transmission of information between cells by depleting the amount of transmitter substance, while too little of the enzyme would have the opposite effect. In addition, we now know that the number of receptor sites can vary: If a particular subsystem becomes overactive, spilling out too much of a particular transmitter, then decreases in the number of receptor sites can bring the system back into equilibrium. Conversely, an increase in the number of receptor sites might mean that a particular stream of messages becomes strengthened. It is easy to see how alterations in any of these delicate microstructures could lead to the aberrant behavior that we call mental illness. Moreover, it is upon these structures that various drugs that affect behavior work, and we are beginning to understand some of these effects in greater detail.

■

The nervous system is thus a general system for modulating experience and behavior. If we are interested in finding a predisposition toward phobias, however, we must look for a more specific system that controls fear and anxiety.

The development of anti-anxiety agents has shed some light on this system. In this line of investigation, two elements were important—the effects of the drugs on humans, particularly upon those suffering from excessive anxiety; and the effects of the same drugs upon the behavior of animals placed in situations that we might consider to be anxiety-provoking.

There are two main classes of drugs that reduce anxiety in humans, the *barbiturates* and the *benzodiazepines*. Intriguingly, both of these compounds have three effects: anti-anxiety, sedative-hypnotic, and anticonvulsant. The barbiturates were first introduced in 1903 following the synthesis of barbituric acid from uric acid. Later work resulted in the development of a family of pharmacological agents, including phenobarbital and Seconal, varying in the duration and rapidity of their action. However, the addictive properties of the barbiturates limited their usefulness in the attempted breakthrough of the anxiety disorders.

Librium, the first of a series of benzodiazepines, was introduced in 1960. Since that time a related agent has appeared every two or three years. These tranquilizers, at first hailed with enthusiasm because of their anti-anxiety effects, later caused widespread alarm because of their addictive properties and their excessive prescription by physicians. In the mid-1970s, it was pointed out that if their use continued to increase at the rate then prevailing, the whole of the American population would be tranquilized by the turn of the century. In response to such alarm, there was a reversal of the trend toward prescribing these compounds, and their use has begun to drop. These considerations are, however, quite secondary to our investigation of the benzodiazepines; they have, by happenstance, thrown much light upon the biochemistry of anxiety and its relief.

In a typical experiment to investigate the anti-anxiety effects of drugs, an animal that has been taught to perform a repetitive behavior, such as pressing a lever to obtain an occasional morsel of food, would be faced with a novel stimulus, or would receive a mild electric shock when pressing the lever. Such an event disrupts the ongoing steady lever-pressing behavior. Now comes a leap of faith! Observation of these animals when behavioral disruption occurs suggests that they are fearful. The animals may freeze, run all over the place, defecate, and so on. Administration of an anti-anxiety drug in a suitable dosage before the experiment counters the fear response; even in the face of mild electric shocks, the animal will persist in pressing the lever.

If the behavior described above actually represents anxiety, and anti-anxiety agents such as the benzodiazepines decrease such behaviors, then we must conclude that when an animal is faced with an un-anticipated—and apparently alarming—situation, its ongoing behavior is probably stopped by the activation of an inhibitory mechanism in the brain. Remember that the phobic demonstrates similar disruption of ongoing behavior upon encountering the feared situation. Such an inhibitory mechanism would obviously be adaptive, perhaps preserving an animal from sudden danger by inhibiting further exploration. Such protection is very much what we postulated as the protective function of common fears.

We can deduce that the benzodiazepines deactivate this inhibitory mechanism, but we need to know exactly how these drugs function in the brain. A second line of research exploring the chemical pathways by which the drug works provides some answers. In 1977, two research groups reported the existence of specific receptor sites in the brain with an affinity for benzodiazepines. This was a remarkable discovery, suggesting that there may be naturally occurring chemical substances in the human brain with an anti-anxiety action, and with a structure very similar to that of the benzodiazepine molecule. No such compound has yet been identified, but vigorous research has already shed light upon the nature of the benzodiazepine receptor site and upon some of the mechanisms involved in the modulation of fear and anxiety.

There seem to be three specific "docking" areas on the benzodiazepine receptor site. The first of these is for the benzodiazepine molecule with its anti-anxiety effects. The second is for compounds that appear to cause anxiety in animals, the effects of which are blocked by administration of the benzodiazepines. The third is for a group of substances that themselves have no active pharmacological effect when administered to animals or to humans but which block the effects of both the benzodiazepines and the anxiety-provoking compounds. The identification of these three receptor sites suggests that there are substances secreted in the brain that lead to the experience of fear and anxiety and other substances that block this effect. Their precise ratio may lead either to the emotionally stable or to the nervous individual.

The anxiety-provoking compounds with a high affinity for the benzodiazepine receptor site were first administered to rodents, but without effect. When administered to primates, however, these same compounds produced startling effects. The monkeys became restless, their hair stood on end, they chattered and screamed. In addition, their heart rate showed a steep increase, very similar to that seen in human panic, and all the stress hormones showed marked and rapid increases. It was found that these effects could be attenuated by the administration of a benzodiazepine.

How does benzodiazepine reduce anxiety? Activation of the benzodiazepine receptor site by one of the benzodiazepines leads to the secretion of an inhibitory neurotransmitter called gamma aminobutyric acid, or GABA. The question then becomes: What action does GABA inhibit?

The answer to this question derives from another line of research, namely the tracing of pathways from one area of the brain to another, either by making small lesions and observing their effects, or by stimulating a particular area of the brain. Such experiments all suggest that a particular part of the "old brain," the septo-hippocampal region, receives messages from the benzodiazepine receptor sites. The old brain, which regulates many vital physiological functions such as body temperature and respiration, forms an increasingly large portion of the brain as we descend the evolutionary ladder. In humans, it is the "new brain"—the cerebral cortex, the organ that allows for thought and reflection—that dominates. But the old brain, now much overshadowed, persists in humans with all its basic functions that have been built in over vast periods of time in our evolutionary development. Among those functions is the fear response. Lesions made in this part of the brain (the septo-hippocampal region) mimic the effects of a tranquilizing agent blunting the fear response; stimulation mimics the effects of anxiety, setting off the alarm signal.

This area, the old brain, seems to act as a comparator, matching incoming information about the environment, which is processed in the cerebral cortex, with expected events in the form of memories of previous experiences, also laid down in the cerebral cortex. If expectations and events match up, the septo-hippocampal region simply operates in a checking mode. If, however, there is a mismatch, then this area takes over control of ongoing behavior and inhibits it.

Such a process is exactly the mechanism that can explain fearful behavior. Faced with an unexpected event, perceived as threatening, ongoing behavior is disrupted and the individual freezes. This excellent protective mechanism is set in motion by the septo-hippocampal comparator. Oversensitivity of this apparatus would evidence itself in a "nervous" disposition, causing a person to freeze or jump at every novel event. The benzodiazepines, by stimulating GABA, inhibit the action of the comparator and blunt the disruption of the ongoing behavioral sequence, thus allowing approach to a novel situation to continue. This was exactly the effect of benzodiazepines in the animal experiments that we reviewed earlier. Under the influence of the tranquilizer, animals continue their behavior even when being shocked.

Given the action of the central comparator, we might expect that individuals who had experienced panic in various situations would halt further approach to any of these situations. Those who had suffered panic attacks under many different circumstances would be the most inhibited—which is exactly what we see when panic becomes a full-blown syndrome associated with agoraphobia.

■

So far we have been considering learning and biological processes as though they were completely separate phenomena. From the scientist's view this is certainly true, for the areas of interest of the two fields are quite different, as are the scientific methods. Within the brain cell, however, they are joined. One of the first demonstrations of this principle occurred in the study of a simple organism, *Aplysia*, a sea snail.

Just as with humans, for example Watson's little Albert, so the sea snail can learn to avoid a particular signal in the environment. The method of conditioning is almost exactly the same as that used by Watson. The sea snail is a vegetarian that eats only seaweed. It can, however, recognize chemicals given off by the juice of a shrimp. In the baseline of the experiment, the sea snail's behavior in the presence of shrimp juice is observed. The little animal ignores the stimulus. Then, a brief electrical shock is delivered to the sea snail's head in the presence of the shrimp juice; this is exactly analogous to Watson's creating a loud noise while little Albert was watching the white rat. After several pairings, the sea snail behaves just like the baby—in the presence of the shrimp juice the animal retreats. Here we have a mini-phobia developed through learning. This is not particularly surprising, since the ability to learn to avoid potentially harmful environmental events is just as adaptive for the sea snail as it is for the human being.

The sea snail's nervous system is much simpler than our own, but the transmission of signals, which are activated when the electric shock is applied, from the skin to the motor system that moves the animal away from the shock has been well mapped out, not only anatomically, but also chemically. It turns out that the release of the neurotransmitter takes place in exactly the same way as it does in the human cell, although the structure of the transmitter is slightly different. Changes in electrical potential cause calcium to flow into the cell, and the vesicles containing the transmitter then migrate to an active zone on the cell surface, where they are loaded into discharge sites and their contents spilled outside the cell. These active zones are contained in small swellings on the cell surface. Amazingly, the number of active zones within these swellings changes as a result of learning. After the conditioning has been completed, there is a 50 percent increase in the number of swellings containing active zones. This increase can in turn facilitate the release of a greater number of vesicles and a larger amount of neurotransmitter. Learning has changed the structure of the nervous system.

What may be happening is that learning changes the genetic structure of cells within the central nervous system. Each cell in the body contains exactly the same genetic material; cells differentiate because certain genes become active while the rest are shut off. It seems possible that learning, and the subsequent chemical changes that occur, cause specific inactivated genes to become active, leading to the changes in structure that take place within the cells of the sea snail's nervous system. When a particular behavior is unlearned, these changes are reversed. If we can extrapolate from the simple brain of the sea snail to the infinitely more complex human brain, then we might have some idea of why phobias persist, since learning leads to structural changes at a very basic level of organization.

■

Fear and anxiety are not, of course, felt in the brain. Rather, they are experienced as changes in visceral and muscular sensation—perhaps a racing heart, stomach cramps, tense muscles, headache, and so on. These changes, as we have seen, may be interpreted by different individuals as signs of impending illness, a heart attack, or perhaps a nervous breakdown.

As illustrated in Figure 5-2, the phobic object or situation is perceived as threatening, and this perception, based upon experience, activates the central anxiety-control mechanisms that we have been examining.

A myriad of electrochemical changes take place as the perception of potential danger is appraised in the cerebral cortex and routed into the subcortical structures comprising the "old brain" in order to alert the autonomic nervous system. The latter great pathway of nervous connections influences many of our bodily functions by acting upon glands and visceral muscles throughout the body to produce the peripheral physiological responses to the feared event. Activation of this system, which forms one aspect of internal regulation, is beyond voluntary control. The autonomic nervous system exerts its effects by

FIGURE 5-2
The Fear Response

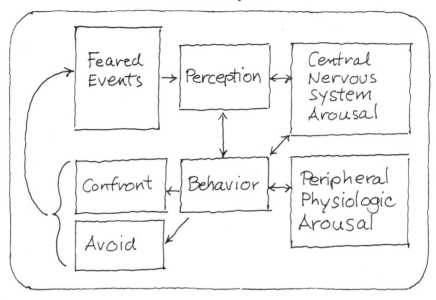

the synergistic action of its two branches, the sympathetic and the parasympathetic, which tend toward opposite actions. If the sympathetic branch, for example, is activated and leads to a contraction of a blood vessel, the parasympathetic branch will lessen its efforts to dilate the same vessel.

As in the brain cell, which we have already examined in some detail, electrical impulses are converted to chemical messengers and back again in complex subsystems at every level of the central and peripheral nervous system. When the adrenal glands, which sit upon the kidneys, are stimulated, a hormone—adrenaline—is poured into the bloodstream. This chemical substance performs several functions, some of which are to speed the heart, raise the blood pressure, and contract blood vessels in the gut, thereby helping to shunt blood to the muscles as they are tensed for action. This is the main outline of the way in which the central and peripheral nervous systems are involved in the fear response. We should note that pleasant circumstances conducive to relaxation will have the opposite effects, hence the cold hands of fear, and the warm hands of pleasure and repose.

The next step in this chain of events is some form of action. In the case of the phobic, the action is usually avoidance. Such avoidance, in turn, allows the fear response to diminish, and the resulting relief tends to reinforce the avoidance behavior. (As we shall see in the next chapter, there are better ways of coping with feared and phobic situations than avoidance, although the initial cost of changing such behavior may be increased discomfort.) It is this continual interplay between the environment, perception, the central and peripheral nervous systems, and behavior that determines fearfulness.

Interestingly, a further feedback mechanism exists; there is evidence that the secretion of adrenaline in response to fear enhances the learning of avoidance behavior. In an experiment testing this notion, rats were anesthetized and subjected to the pairing of a mild noise and an electric shock under one of two conditions—either following an injection of adrenaline or following an injection of saline. Ten days later, while drinking water, the animals were tested for their response to the sound. Animals who had received adrenaline showed far greater avoidance behavior—in this instance, a cessation of drinking—in response to the noise than did those who had received only saline.

Transposing these findings to the human phobic situation, it seems likely that the association of the feared event, the unpleasant visceral response, and the secretion of adrenaline would lead to more rapid learning of avoidance behavior. In more general terms, such enhanced learning would be adaptive, since the more dangerous the situation the stronger would be the future avoidance of it.

■

We are now in a position to piece together what we have learned from the various approaches to fears and phobias that we have examined so far and to develop a more comprehensive theory of their origins, before moving on to consider treatment. As we have seen, phobia arises upon the base of an inbuilt mechanism designed to protect both animals and humans from adverse aspects of the environment. Fear, it seems, has been arranged as an early warning system that helps the individual to avoid potentially dangerous situations; pain, on the other hand, warns of immediate harm—the hand-on-the-hot-stove response. While pain leads to a reflex withdrawal of the affected part—pulling the hand away from the stove—fear leads to a withdrawal of the whole organism from the situation, often in children to the safety of a parent. Separation fear is the first line of defense; if this is breached, then animal and injury fears come into play; finally, pain warns of imminent physical danger.

The ability to supplement the operation of the innate fear response by means of experience confers an enormous advantage upon both animals and humans, allowing a more flexible adaptation to a novel and changing environment. New avoidances can be learned by associating an event that gives rise to some form of physiological disturbance with a previously neutral circumstance, a method of learning called "conditioning," that is the same both for very simple animals and for humans. More complex modes of learning play a part in the case of humans, and thoughts and memories intensify learned fears.

Learning interacts with biology within the cells of the nervous system. One likely point of interaction, as we have seen from research with the sea snail, is at the end of a sensory neuron. Here, avoidance learning results in an increase in the number of active zones at which a neurotransmitter is released. It seems likely that a similar mechanism takes place in humans. The release of neurotransmitters in avoidance learning may well affect the benzodiazepine receptor site, which in turn affects the setting of the comparator mechanism in the old brain, either diminishing or increasing avoidance behavior. The setting of this system could also be modified by inheritance; some people may be predisposed to increased fearfulness. It would be at this level that the genetic association between depression and phobia would be expressed, although the mechanism underlying this association has not been elucidated. The interactive influences of learning and biology, in turn, might make fear acquisition more rapid in some individuals than in others, and might also delay the normal unlearning of the common fears that occurs with experience, so that fears would be turned into phobias.

Why panic should not be associated with the simple phobias is less clear, unless we postulate that the primary role of separation anxiety in protecting the very young requires a more intimate association of this defensive behavior with the general alarm system than do the injury fears that would affect a somewhat older child. Activation of separation anxiety in the infant would cause a marked physiological arousal, accompanied by cries of alarm aimed at rapidly drawing maternal attention to the plight of the infant. The more mobile older child would be able to run away from the dangerous situation, and separation anxiety and alarm would only be activated if the child could not flee the danger. The phobias deriving from a prolongation of separation anxiety would then tend to activate the general fear response causing panic, while those deriving from other fear clusters would cause fear and avoidance behavior.

Given this model of the acquisition of phobias in general and of the panic syndrome in particular, we can now turn to treatment. Our model suggests that both chemical agents and methods aimed at altering what has been learned could be used to modify phobic behavior. The next three chapters will consider these two treatment strategies.

THE QUEST FOR A CURE: FIRST STEPS 6

The search for an effective psychological treatment of phobia dramatically affected the practice of psychotherapy, challenged existing therapeutic theories, and set new standards for research. The development of this research effort provides an excellent example of the way in which clinical scientists build study upon study in the search for safe and effective treatment of a particular condition. As in a good detective story, there are false starts, red herrings, and ultimately the correct reading of the clues that lie scattered about. But there is a difference: The answer leads not to an ending, but to a new beginning. Until a disorder is eliminated—an extraordinarily rare event in the history of medicine—the search for an improved treatment cannot be stopped.

■

The public has a right to know how well a particular therapy has been tested. The questions, Is it safe? Is it effective? Will it work for my particular problem? How sure are you? What are the alternatives? should be asked by all patients when a course of treatment is proposed. The clinician should be able to answer such questions by reference to an adequate experimental literature. At any one time, the "state of the art" therapy for a given condition may be debatable. But all too often, prejudice and what the therapist was taught many years ago, rather than recent scientific developments, may determine the therapy selected. Therapists should be familiar enough with all the pertinent studies to discuss them with patients, and patients should not be inhibited about asking questions. Many procedures used in medicine have not been sufficiently tested, and the buyer should beware.

Ideally, the development of a therapy should follow the pattern shown in the accompanying diagram (see Figure 6-1). Beginning with a clinical observation—the classic bedside insight of the physician—or with an idea derived from an observation or theory in one of the basic sciences, in this instance, psychology, a new therapy is devised. This therapy is then tested in a series of patients with the disorder. During this early phase, problems in the application of the new therapy can be detected and corrected, and a standard treatment protocol in which the new findings are adapted to the realities of the clinical situation can be devised.

If the therapy appears to promise better results than existing therapies, it should then be subjected to a series of controlled studies in which it is compared either with no treatment or with the best prevailing treatment. Two conditions are essential for such clinical trials: Patients should be allocated at random to one or another of the treatments, and objective measures of outcome should be used. The first clinical trials are short-term; they should be followed by long-term trials, with follow-up of patients for a year or more. Because long-term studies are expensive and time-consuming, they are relatively rare. But a long-term study is a critical step in the evaluation of a new therapy; if all its therapeutic advantages are found to disappear at the end of a year, it would have to offer other advantages, such as fewer deleterious side effects, or lower costs, to justify its adoption in clinical practice. Along the way, unexpected problems or new discoveries may lead to the emergence of alternative modes of therapy, again to be tested against the original. And so the process repeats itself, ensuring the development of improved treatments, until no further improvement is possible. In the case of phobia, particularly the agoraphobia-panic syndrome, research is presently in a very active phase, as it focuses on refining the two different approaches to treatment, the psychological and the pharmacological.

■

Although, as we shall see, the experimental work leading to the evolution of modern psychological therapies for fears and phobias began following World War II, earlier attempts had been made. In the 1920s, Mary Cover Jones, a young psychologist working at Teachers College, Columbia University, was impressed with Watson's work in understanding the development of children's fears and decided that

FIGURE 6-1
The Research Progression

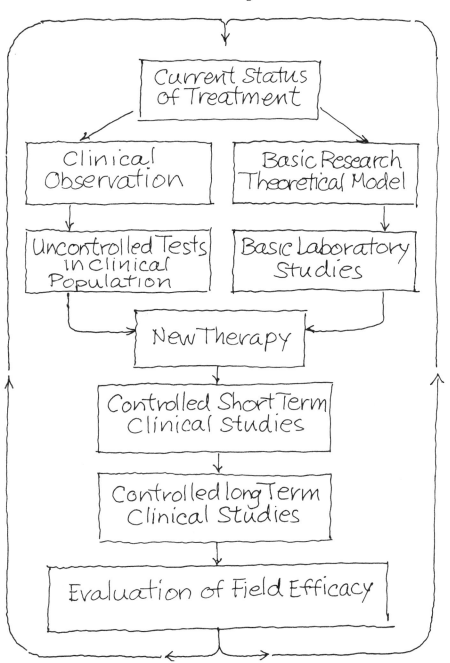

"a study of how children's fears may be reduced or eradicated should be the next point of attack."[10]

Working in an institution for the temporary care of children, she systematically examined the children for various kinds of fears by exposing them to darkness, to being left alone, to a snake, a white rat, a rabbit, and so on. Then she tried by various methods, none of which was effective, to diminish the fears. She found, for example, that neglect did not work, that the notion that fears will die out if left alone could not be confirmed. Although we now know that fears—particularly childhood fears—may die out over years, Jones correctly observed that they do not disappear over weeks or months. In every case, the fears continued unabated.

Next, Jones tried talking with the children about their fear, connecting the feared object with pleasant stories. If they were afraid of a rabbit, then she read *Peter Rabbit* to them. A child would often say, "Where is your rabbit? Show me your rabbit," but at the sight of the rabbit the child was as frightened as ever. Although the children had learned to speak freely about rabbits, their fears had not changed.

Two methods did seem to work. The first of these involved pairing an *actual*, rather than *described*, feared object, with a pleasant experience such as eating. One child was given candies, while the rabbit of which he was afraid was placed nearby. At first this situation provoked crying, but soon the child was playing with the animal. Similarly, when a child with a fear observed children who were unafraid playing with the animal, his fears and avoidance were eliminated. Jones interpreted the successful results of both methods as demonstrating the power of a pleasurable experience to overcome a fearful experience.

But the time was not ripe. Jones's work languished in the scientific journals, only to be rediscovered when her ideas fitted better with prevailing notions of causation and cure. Any idea, however sound, has to be introduced at the right time to be adopted. Jones was thirty years ahead of her time.

■

In 1947, having spent some time reading and reflecting on therapies for phobia and on the prevailing psychological theories, Joseph Wolpe, a South African psychiatrist, began a series of animal experiments. These experiments would, in the end, lead to a superior therapy for fears and phobias. Working from current psychological theories of learning—theories that had been developed from experimental work over the preceding quarter-century—Wolpe conducted an experiment with cats, first generating and then treating phobias in these animals. To do this, he would place the cat in a cage with a floor through which an electric current could be passed, a current that was "very uncomfortable to the human hand, but not productive of tissue damage." Aware that the very room in which the experiment was carried out, and even the experimenter himself, were part of the setting, Wolpe moved the cage from room to room, each one a little different from the others.

Just as in Watson's experiment with little Albert, the first order of business was to see whether the cats would react to being in a cage in any or all of the various rooms, or to the sound of a hooter, which was to be used in the experiment. The cats' reactions to both the cage and the hooter were "inconsequential." The next step was to shock the cats and to sound the hooter simultaneously. In each case the reaction was the same. After a few exposures to the shock, even though no further shocks were given, the cats displayed "neurotic symptoms" whenever they were placed in the cage—either extreme restlessness, accompanied by rapid breathing, crying, and batting their heads against the cage (in an effort to escape?), or tense immobility. When the hooter was sounded, the symptoms became worse. Symptoms also appeared outside the experimental situation, particularly in the presence of the experimenter, but were less pronounced in those rooms that were most unlike that in which the original shock had been given. These behaviors very much resemble phobic behavior in adults.

Wolpe now used his "theory of reciprocal inhibition" to treat this neurotic behavior. While his idea was almost identical to that of Mary Cover Jones, Wolpe stated it in neurophysiological rather than psychological terms. Briefly stated, the theory supposes that the nervous system cannot be both relaxed and anxious at the same time, because these responses are innervated by different and incompatible branches of the nervous system.

To produce relaxation, he fed the cats, first in a room least like that in which the shock had been administered. As the feeding progressed from day to day, the neurotic behavior diminished until the cat was quite comfortable in that setting. Then feeding was begun in a room a little more like the one in which the animal had initially received the shock; and so on, until the cat was no longer nervous in any situation. But if the hooter was now sounded the cat relapsed. Every aspect of the induced phobia had to be treated! Wolpe now fed the cat with the hooter sounding, first either for a very short time, or very softly, and then gradually increasing the duration or the level of sound. Again the fear response disappeared—this time forever.

Now came a great conceptual leap. Wolpe applied his therapeutic method to cases of human phobias, but not by feeding his subjects in order to relax them. He taught his patients a muscular relaxation technique and then had them *imagine* their feared situations rather than *creating* the direct experience *for* them. These were major changes in the experimental protocol. The new therapy, which he called "systematic desensitization," produced impressive results. When applied to a large series of phobic patients, for whom the outcome was carefully documented, some 80 percent were rated as "cured" and another 10 percent as "much improved." The question that arises is: How good are these results? Luckily, the Berlin Psychoanalytic Institute had published figures for the psychoanalytic treatment of phobia. Their results showed between 40 and 60 percent "cured" or "much improved." When another large series of patients was treated with briefer psychotherapy, the results also suggested that about 60 percent would be "cured" or "much improved." The comparison of these results with 90 percent for his systematic desensitization led Wolpe to the justifiable conclusion that systematic desensitization was better than the prevailing treatment. As he put it,

> It is obvious that if the reciprocal inhibition principle is indeed a master key to the cure of neurosis, a much brighter future lies before the world's victims of neurotic suffering. But in a matter like this, conviction cannot be founded on one man's experience. The proposition must be put to the test by others.[11]

The time was right for a new therapy for neurotic disorders, although the ensuing ideological battle would be vigorous. One trend was already in motion: Dissatisfaction with the results of psychoanalytic therapy, as well as with the lack of acceptable research into its efficacy, was growing. This opened the door for a new therapy. Wolpe had put his foot in the door, and he and his followers eventually established behavior therapy as an alternative to psychoanalysis. The second trend could not have been foreseen but was probably equally important: It was discovered that the very common human fear of snakes was an excellent model for phobia, allowing for an abundance of laboratory investigations of the new therapy and the setting of new standards for psychotherapy research.

■

A neophyte looking at our mental health system might conclude that most psychotherapy was directed toward changing the scores on paper and pencil tests such as the Minnesota Multiphasic Personality Inventory (MMPI), a compilation of several hundred questions about various aspects of mental health. Yet we know that coming up with "more normal" answers on a multiple choice examination is not the aim of treatment; rather, treatment is directed toward useful *behavior* change. So why not measure behavior change directly? Oddly enough, at mid-century this idea was still considered radical. Only with the introduction of behavior therapy was specificity in the *measurement* of outcome regarded as important and *objective* measurement regarded as essential. It is fitting that the very first controlled study of systematic desensitization used a *behavioral* measure to verify the self-report of the patients involved.

In this pioneering study, conducted by a South African psychologist in 1959, two groups of phobics, one made up of people who suffered primarily from fears of heights, the other from fears of enclosed places, were allocated at random either to systematic desensitization or to interpretive psychotherapy. Both treatments were carried out in a group setting. In the desensitization group, the patients were first taught to relax, and then to imagine various scenes depicting a gradual approach to their feared situations until they no longer experienced anxiety.

At the end of therapy, all patients who claimed to be cured of their fears of heights and enclosed places were asked to face their feared situation. In one such test the height phobics, for example, were asked to climb to the third landing of a fire escape, a height of about fifty feet; from there they went by elevator to the eighth floor of the building, where they were asked to count the number of automobiles passing by on the road below. (Only two persons who claimed to be cured failed this dizzying task, and were duly counted as failures.)

The overall results were decisive: for desensitization, thirteen recoveries and five failures; for psychotherapy only two recoveries and fifteen failures—a very significant difference in outcome. We must remember, however, that these results were for the treatment of relatively simple phobias; as more severe phobias were treated, the lead of desensitization over psychotherapy narrowed.

In another study, in which the majority of patients suffered from the agoraphobia-panic syndrome, systematic desensitization was compared with both group and individual psychotherapy. The results of this study were quite straightforward. Treatment with desensitization lasted for nine months, individual psychotherapy for one year, and group psychotherapy for eighteen months. After six months of treatment, those treated with desensitization had improved more than those receiving individual psychotherapy, who, in turn, tended to have an advantage over those receiving group psychotherapy. Eighteen months after the beginning of treatment, however, the differences were less marked; those treated with psychotherapy had now caught up with those treated with behavior therapy. Since behavior therapy required fewer sessions than psychotherapy to achieve comparable results, it proved less costly to the patient and therefore should be the preferred approach to the agoraphobia-panic syndrome. We must, however, ask whether the two therapies might have some common factor responsible for the improvement, albeit at different rates. At the time no one asked this question, and the next step involved the laboratory study of phobia, using snake-fearful volunteers.

■

What were psychologists doing in the 1960s, scaring women undergraduates with snakes? And without arousing any complaints! The answer is that they were taking psychotherapy research into the laboratory, where desensitization could be studied at greater leisure, and in greater detail, than was possible in the clinical setting.

In 1960, using snake fears as an experimental model of phobia, Peter Lang devised an experiment to test some of the theoretical assumptions of behavior therapy and psychoanalysis. Psychoanalytic theory suggests that there would be little change in a symptom, such as a snake fear, unless the symbolic meaning—the snake is usually considered as a sexual symbol—is identified and the various meanings and implications for the patient's life are worked through. On the other hand, Wolpe had suggested that fears and phobias could be unlearned by a much simpler process—by substituting relaxation for anxiety.

Lang devised a simple experimental design. The young women who were afraid of snakes were allocated at random: Some received no treatment; others systematic desensitization. Each was brought into a room where a small boa constrictor was lying in a cage on a table in plain sight. The experimenter invited the subject to come closer to the cage, to touch the cage outside and inside, to touch the snake, to pick it up. Naturally, the snake-fearful women would usually not approach the cage, and the distance they left between themselves and the cage could be measured off to give an index of fearfulness.

Those allocated to the treatment group were then trained in deep muscle relaxation. To induce relaxation, groups of muscles are first tensed—in the arm, for example, by making a fist for a few seconds— and are then quickly relaxed. Each group of muscles throughout the body is relaxed in turn, and with each new group the feeling of relaxation deepens. Particular attention is paid to breathing, developing slow rhythmic respiration, and feeling the sensation of deepening relaxation as each breath is expelled. Intrusive thoughts are ignored, and relaxation may be deepened by imagining one's self in a pleasant situation, such as lying in the sun on a beach. With a little practice, most people can achieve a sense of deep relaxation. When an individual is relaxed, any anxiety provoked by imagining of a fear-arousing scene quickly dissipates.

Each participant in the study drew up an individualized hierarchy of her snake fears, perhaps beginning with imagining the word "snake," pictures of a snake, or visiting the zoo, and progressing through to visualizing herself actually picking up a harmless snake. Each was asked to list twenty items in her hierarchy. Sixteen sessions of therapy were given, five to learn muscular relaxation and to develop the hierarchy and eleven for the desensitization. In the treatment session, the subjects would first be relaxed and then be asked briefly to imagine their least feared scene. This would be repeated several times until there was no residual anxiety. Then the next scene would be tackled. Some subjects completed their hierarchy during treatment, others barely got going by the last session.

Once more the results were clear. Seven of thirteen young women in the desensitization group could actually hold the snake at the final test. And six months after the experiment, their fear of snakes had not returned! Those who had completed all sixteen sessions of therapy did much better at the final test than those who had not. Of the eleven in the control (untreated) group, only two could hold the snake—a significant difference. These results support Wolpe's theory, rather than psychoanalytic theory. As the investigators concluded,

It is not necessary to explore the factors contributing to the learning of a phobia, or its "unconscious meaning" in order to eliminate it. . . . In reducing phobic behavior it is not necessary to change the "personality as a whole." People can unlearn their fears, just as they learn and unlearn other things.[12]

So far, then, it appeared that desensitization was more efficient than psychotherapy in the case of more complex phobias, and superior to psychotherapy in the treatment of simple phobias. In addition, the research findings favored Wolpe's learning theory rather than psychoanalytic theory. But findings from other studies began to raise questions about the actual process by which desensitization leads to improvement. One of these exploited the laboratory study of snake fears in a novel way in order to identify the action of subcomponents of the therapy.

■

It has long been known that one ingredient common to all therapies is the engendering of a positive expectancy of outcome by means of therapeutic suggestion or instruction. This element of therapy, partly responsible for "the placebo effect," is what binds together modern medicine and the witch doctor. Both therapeutic systems offer a believable rationale for their effectiveness and suggest that the treatment will work. Such rationales are culturally specific, and thus a given therapy may not always be transferable from one culture to another. This observation laid the groundwork for a study carried out by my colleagues and myself with snake-fearful young women. The women were allocated at random to one of two groups. The groups were treated identically, except that one group thought they were taking part in an experiment studying the physiological effects of visualizing snake scenes, while the other group was told that they were being treated for their snake fear.

Both groups were taught relaxation, and both worked through a standard fear hierarchy in exactly the same way. To complete the deception, participants in both groups were attached to a polygraph that measured physiological responses to the visualizing of feared scenes. The difference in what they believed to be the purpose of desensitization had a profound effect on the ability of these students to approach a snake at the end of the experiment. Those who believed they were receiving therapy improved more than twice as much as those who believed they were taking part in an experiment to measure snake fears. Indeed, those in the latter group were not significantly different at the end of the experiment from a control group who had received no treatment; the lack of a positive expectancy had almost completely neutralized the effect of desensitization.

This experiment, while not fatal for Wolpe's theory, suggests that the pairing of a fear-arousing scene with relaxation does not *always* lead to the unlearning of fear. This observation led us to make a more crucial test of the theory, namely to omit relaxation from desensitization therapy. This should have completely abolished the effectiveness of therapy, yet it did not. When relaxation was no longer paired with the visualizing of fear-arousing scenes, patients with simple phobias improved just as much as they did when relaxation was used. The obvious conclusion is that relaxation is not essential to the treatment and that desensitization works in a way different from that postulated by Wolpe. But how it worked was not obvious, and as we shall see in the next chapter the answer to this riddle was to come from a new line of research.

THE QUEST FOR A CURE: EXPOSURE THERAPY 7

B. F. Skinner, one of the most important contributors to the science of psychology, made the simple yet fundamental discovery that behavior is influenced by its effect on the environment. If a behavior results in a reward of some kind, the action tends to persist. If, on the other hand, punishment results, then the behavior tends to disappear. These findings, some of them quite complex, apply to all organisms, from the amoeba to the human being. We have already seen an example of learning of this kind in the sea snail. Given the universally applicable nature of these principles of learning, it made good sense to apply them to a variety of abnormal behaviors, and again it was found that the learning and unlearning of many abnormal behaviors followed the same rules. The next step was to apply these procedures to phobics.

The first of our patients to take part in these experiments was a young woman who, shortly after she married, found herself unable to leave home. Even walking a few yards from her front door terrified her and often led to panic; she felt she might faint, choke, or even die if she did not return home at once. This phobia could be traced back to her childhood. She was her mother's favorite, perhaps because she was the only girl in the family, a previous baby girl having died after a brief and mysterious illness. Her mother hovered over her second daughter, fearing that she too might be taken from her. As the young girl grew up, she found this attention comforting, but also irritating, for many restrictions were placed upon her to "keep her safe."

When the patient was eleven years old, her mother, who had for some time been complaining of a choking sensation, was suddenly hospitalized for thyroid surgery. Frightened by her mother's illness and imagining that her mother might die, she herself began to avoid eating solid foods, fearing that she might "choke to death." Here we can examine the development of the hypochondriacal fears seen in adults with agoraphobia and can appreciate how closely linked to fears of separation—in this case, by death—such symptoms are. The child's fear of choking, as we might expect, gradually dissipated when her mother returned from the hospital, but she remained afraid of being separated from her mother and never, for example, stayed overnight with friends.

It is not surprising, then, that this young woman found herself unable to function independently after leaving home to marry. Her inability to leave her new home was reinforced by an increasing dependence on her husband and by the solicitous overconcern of her mother, who was more and more frequently called in to stay with her. Her disability in a mobile society was enormous, and since she was cut off from her friends and from so much enjoyment in the outside world, depression added to her misery. Several years of psychotherapy brought her no relief, and she eventually became addicted to sleeping pills, which she discovered gave her enough courage to venture a little way alone. Eventually, she came to our laboratory for help.

To measure the patient's improvement, we laid out a mile-long course from the hospital to downtown, marked at about 25-yard intervals. Before beginning the experiment, we asked the patient to walk as far as she could along the course. Each time she balked at the front door of the hospital. Then the first phase of the experiment began: We held two sessions each day in which the patient was praised for staying out of the hospital for a longer and longer time. The reinforcement schedule was simple. If the patient stayed outside for 20 seconds on one trial and then on the next attempt stayed out for 30 seconds, she was praised enthusiastically. Now, however, the criterion for praise was raised—without the patient's knowledge—to 25 seconds. If she met the criterion she was again praised, and the time was increased again. If she did not stay out long enough, the therapist simply ignored her performance. To gain the therapist's attention, which she valued, she had to stay out longer each time.

This she did, until she was able to stay out for almost half an hour. But was she walking farther each time? Not at all. She was simply circling around in the front drive of the hospital, keeping the "safe place" in sight at all times. We therefore changed the reinforcement to reflect the distance walked. Now she began to walk farther and farther each time. Supported by this simple therapeutic procedure, the patient was progressively able to increase her self-confidence. The crucial question now became: What would happen if the reinforcement was stopped, if the therapist no longer praised the patient's progress?

Two things happened when praise was stopped. The patient at first walked farther, almost doubling her previous distance to reach a point within sight of downtown. Then, after a few sessions, she became increasingly less capable of walking alone, and her phobia completely returned. This phenomenon is well-known in reinforcement experiments as the "extinction burst." Animals pressing a lever for an occasional food reward will redouble their efforts temporarily if food is discontinued. Here the same thing was happening with a very complex piece of human behavior. This reversal of progress demonstrated that improvement depended upon reinforcement, a conclusion that was strengthened when praise was begun once more, for soon the patient was able to walk downtown alone. Praise was then thinned out, but slowly, and the patient was encouraged to walk anywhere she pleased. Five years later, she was still perfectly well. We might assume that the benefits of being more independent maintained the gains and compensated for the loss of praise from the therapist.

Another aspect of this experiment is worth underlining. For the first time, a patient's phobic symptoms came under the control of a therapist. No longer was the symptom fluctuating at random during the course of therapy, as is so often the case. By systematically changing a single factor in the patient's environment, the therapist's behavior, the symptoms could be made to come and go.

As with all research, what goes wrong can be as interesting as what goes right. Although we found that a number of patients overcame their severe phobic symptoms in response to this same simple treatment, others improved before we began to use reinforcement—while we were simply measuring the extent of their phobias by seeing how far they could walk alone. This was puzzling, since most of our patients had been disabled for years. Indeed, severe disability was one of the conditions for admission to this experimental program, in which the treatment was free. Evidently some invisible therapeutic factor was at work. Now we had to track it down.

On thinking about the way in which we measured phobic behavior—by placing the phobic in his or her feared situation—it struck us that patients might be able to observe themselves improving and that the measurements would be affected by this factor. If you walk farther on one attempt than on an earlier one, you can observe your achievement. Such environmental feedback is an important element in the learning of many skills and is essential for the mastering of many tasks. Imagine the difficulty a pilot would have in flying an airplane without information from the instrument panel.

Our next experiment involved altering feedback. To do this, we had to find a phobia in which the environment provided poor feedback so that we could ourselves improve or strengthen the feedback and then test the effects. The perfect problem for this experiment turned out to be claustrophobia. Time perception is notoriously poor, particularly if one is anxious. Each claustrophobic was asked to enter a small room alone, and told to come out when anxiety set in. In the first phase of the experiment, we gave each of them a stopwatch and asked them to note how long they were able to stay in the room. In the next phase—removal of a feedback—we told them that the watch was broken. In the final phase, we restored the feedback by returning the watch. Meanwhile, with a timer that was started by the door's closing and stopped by its opening, we could measure how long they were able to stay in the room.

Although these patients all improved during the course of the experiment, the addition of feedback proved only marginally helpful to them. It could not possibly be the unidentified factor responsible for the large gains observed in the experiment measuring how far an agoraphobic patient could walk; her gains had continued in the absence of reinforcement. However, another possibility remained: The measurement of the phobia during our experiments forced the patients into contact with their feared object or situation. Could the exposure itself be therapeutic? So once again we devised a series of experiments to test the influence of a new factor in helping people overcome their fear.

In the first experiment we arranged a fear-provoking situation for a knife phobic. This woman, now middle-aged, had experienced fears of injury for many years, but with little effect upon her functioning. One day she was washing up after dinner as her grandchildren played about her feet. As she was drying the carving knife, and evidently irritated by their noisemaking, the idea came to her that she might stab one of the children. This thought provoked panic, and from that moment on she was unable to look at, let alone use, a knife. Not being able to cook, she began to lose weight, as did her husband. Eventually this weight loss, combined with the suffering, led her to seek treatment.

The experimental situation in this case consisted of a box with a sliding door. Inside the box was a sharp knife, which the patient could see when she opened the door. She was instructed to look at the knife until she felt anxious and then to close the door. Once more a timer automatically recorded how long she was able to look at the knife. Trial by trial she was able to look ever longer at the knife. Now the experiment was halted for several days and all treatment discontinued. Had she continued to improve in this interval, we would have had to credit some factor other than exposure. But, in fact, she remained at precisely the level she had reached when we halted exposure.

Recalling the placebo effect of therapy, we asked: Why should she improve if she no longer believes she is being treated? In order to make sure that actual exposure was the necessary element in effecting improvement, we had to control for the placebo effect by alternating two treatments. For this, we used new patients. The first treatment was practice in facing the feared situation; the second was psychotherapy to try to uncover the source of the phobia. Once more, progress occurred only when patients were exposed to their feared situation and not during the psychotherapy, even though they now *believed* they were being helped.

We had found the missing therapeutic ingredient—exposure to the feared situation. This finding, of course, comes as no surprise to the many parents who have helped their children overcome fears by gradually exposing them to the objects or situations they fear. Nor would it have surprised Freud, who had already noted that there comes a point in the analysis of phobic patients when they must be urged to expose themselves to their feared object. Without such exposure they will not improve. To this, we had added only one fact—the analysis isn't necessary!

Even Wolpe's animal experiments have been shown to work because the animals are systematically *exposed* to the situation they have been taught to fear, and not because eating inhibits fear. As we shall see, systematic desensitization probably works by inducing patients to get out and *expose* themselves to their phobic situation.

■

During the late 1960s, when we were beginning the work that would isolate exposure as the critical procedure in ridding patients of their phobias—and correct our original hypothesis that reinforcement was the critical element—a second route was being taken that would lead to the same conclusion. This route, followed largely by researchers at the Institute of Psychiatry in London, began with the introduction of a dramatic new therapy for phobia. Instead of having patients gradually approach their feared situation in imagination, and inducing relaxation to minimize anxiety, these experimenters asked the patients to imagine strong, even unrealistic phobic scenes and encouraged them to deeply experience every twinge of anxiety that arose. This new therapy, called "implosion therapy" was based upon the notion of extinction, that is, if a feared stimulus is repeatedly presented, the fear and anxiety associated with it should steadily diminish.

Consider, for example, a patient with a fear of heights. In implosion therapy, the patient would be asked to imagine entering an elevator and going up to the top floor of a 40-story building. The apprehension and anxiety caused by this imagined scene would be vividly described and the patient would be asked to experience it as fully as possible. Arriving (in imagination) at the top floor, the patient would then visualize climbing the stairway to the roof garden, walking to the edge of the building, and then looking down at the small people and automobiles passing far below. Suddenly the wall on which he was leaning would crumble and he would begin to fall, grasping at the remains of the masonry. Slowly his fingers would lose their grip, and the long descent would begin. Every sensation on the way down would be vividly described, as would the eventual crash onto the sidewalk, with all its blood and gore. Aspects of the scene that had been particularly fear-arousing would be determined by questioning the patient and would be embellished in the next session. These dramatic presentations would continue until the patient's anxiety disappeared.

Implosion therapy looked very promising when compared with the then standard desensitization therapy. Now, though, came a very muddled interval in the progress toward a reliable therapy. Many investigators could find no difference in outcome among the treatments—desensitization, exposure, and implosion therapy. Eventually, however, the picture cleared. In those studies showing no difference of outcome among therapies, the patients in all the groups studied had practiced confronting their feared situation in the intervals between the treatment sessions. *Once again exposure was the critical factor in treatment and not the other therapeutic procedures.*

In the next series of experiments the role of exposure was further clarified by comparing real and imagined approaches to the phobic situation. In a study carried out in Holland, agoraphobic individuals were assigned at random to implosion therapy, to actual exposure to the feared situation, or to a combination of the two. Exposure to the real-life situation was clearly superior to exposure in imagination or to any other therapy where no direct exposure occurred. Our own work had confirmed this finding. If, on the other hand, direct practice in the feared situation was added to the treatment of patients in other therapies such as desensitization, treatment of those patients became as effective as, but no more effective than, the treatment by exposure alone.

All psychological treatments of phobia, from psychoanalysis to implosion, work to the extent that the patient is motivated to expose himself to his feared situation. The quickest method is demonstrably to have patients directly expose themselves. Encouragement in the form of praise, a gradual approach to the feared situation, and the modeling of fearless behavior—all these have been shown to facilitate therapy, but only to the extent that they facilitate exposure to the feared object or situation.

Exposure therapy has now been used long enough to allow the results of the therapy to be evaluated up to nine years after treatment. Several studies have reported on follow-up periods ranging from four to nine years. They all tell the same story: The initial gains due to treatment are maintained over the entire follow-up period. Measures of the phobia, whether a simple phobia or agoraphobia, are stable over this time, as are measures of anxiety, depression, and social functioning. Psychoanalytic theory would predict that new symptoms should arise if a symptom is removed without the patient's understanding the cause of the original symptom. One study particularly examined this point, concentrating on those patients who had completely recovered; there was no evidence that new symptoms had replaced the vanished phobia.

■

Earlier in this book we saw that ritualistic behavior may serve as a cocoon, helping some phobics to wall themselves off from their feared objects or situations more effectively than is possible by mere avoidance. Something more than exposure therapy would seem to be needed in these cases. The most common compulsions consist of repetitive checking or handwashing; compulsions may, however, take other forms. One of my patients, a ten-year-old girl, was severely handicapped by her rituals. Her illness began with a fear that she might hurt someone; it was precipitated by an incident in which she actually hit a playmate in the face with a baseball bat. The ensuing tears, the fury of the playmate's parents, and the need for the wound to be sewn up in the emergency room—all this was profoundly frightening to my young patient. The roots of this fear may have been fed by her parents' strict religious beliefs, their extremely scrupulous personal relationships with others, and their care always to avoid the actuality or appearance of harming others.

Soon after the accident, the little girl began to limit her activities; at first she avoided playing with other children, then slowed down all her actions so that she could take extra care in order to avoid "hurting anyone or breaking anything." Eventually, her entire day became ritualized. At the start of each day, her clothes had to be laid out in exactly the same way, so that she could put them on with economy of effort. Each limb had to be inserted into each article of clothing in the right manner. If anything was done incorrectly, then the whole process had to begin again. Dressing often took eight hours. Eating was also ritualized and was limited to food that could be swallowed without biting into it, for biting might cause harm. Dressing, eating one meal, and undressing again, took up all day and often stretched into the night. By taking up all her time, these rituals effectively cut her off from normal life, and, of course, from the possibility of harming anyone or anything.

Until quite recently no treatment for compulsions existed. The first glimmer of hope came from an interesting animal experiment in which rats were taught a behavior that looked much like a ritual. A rat would be placed in a cage through the floor of which a painful electric current could be passed. A distinctive signal light would be turned on and the floor electrified ten seconds later. Under these conditions, the rats, very sensibly, would jump all over the cage trying to get away from the pain-inducing floor. If a perch was now provided halfway up one of the walls of the cage, the rat would soon learn to jump up and crouch upon it until the signal light was turned off. And as soon as the light was turned on again, the animal would leap onto the perch once more. Now the electric current could be completely turned off without affecting the rat's behavior, for the animal would continue to jump up and down from the perch in response to the signal light's being turned on or off. To an onlooker, the rat was engaging in a strange ritualistic activity, leaping on and off the perch time after time. Yet the original "feared event," the electrified floor, no longer existed.

This experiment would have remained a mere classroom curiosity were it not for the fact that the researcher went one step further; he discovered that an extraordinarily simple method could cure the compulsion. He removed the perch from the cage. Now, when the rapid signal light was turned on, the rat leaped at the wall only to find no perch. These desperate leaps would continue until the rat discovered that the floor was no longer painful. The compulsion had been cured! Might not a similarly simple procedure help eradicate the infinitely more complex human compulsion?

Luckily this question was taken up by a British psychologist who tested the treatment on a series of patients with compulsive hand-washing rituals. But how to proceed? In the case of the rat, the compulsion was prevented by mechanical means—the removal of the perch. For handwashers, the analogous remedy was to turn off the water for a few days, thus completely preventing the ritual from being performed. This apparently simple maneuver was, however, not without its dangers, at least according to contemporary wisdom; the textbooks warned that removal of a defensive behavior, such as a ritual, might lead to catastrophic consequences—perhaps a breakdown into an even more severe mental illness such as schizophrenia. But given the terrible incapacity of the compulsive patient, and the complete lack of a successful treatment, many patients were willing to take that risk.

When the taps were turned off, as might be expected, many of the patients were frightened and required unusually supportive nursing care. Not one of them, however, showed any tendency to develop a more serious mental illness under the stress of losing their compulsions. After the taps had been turned off for ten days, the question became: What would happen when the patients had free access to water? Would they all relapse into their previous compulsive state? Few of them did. The outcome of this new treatment, called "response prevention," was excellent. The majority of the patients showed substantial improvement; some completely recovered. A promising new therapy seemed to have been discovered.

The next step in the testing of a new treatment is, as we have seen, to conduct a controlled clinical trial. Since no standard treatment for compulsive disorders existed, the proper control was to compare response prevention with a placebo treatment. In one of our experiments, we used saline injections as the placebo, telling the patient

that he was receiving a new drug believed to be effective in controlling compulsions. To measure the amount of time the patient spent washing his hands, we placed a board with microswitches beneath it on the floor surrounding the sink in his hospital room. To wash his hands, he had to stand on the board, thus activating the switches, which in turn started a timer running in another room; when he stepped off the board, the timer would stop.

In the first phase of the experiment we simply observed the amount of handwashing that the patient engaged in. He washed his hands about fifteen times each day, for about forty minutes each time—a total of ten hours a day. Moreover, the length of time that he spent washing his hands increased as the days went by. When we asked the patient about this, he replied that being in a hospital frightened him because it was a place where patients with all sorts of infectious disorders were brought, thus bringing him closer to his fear. Next we gave the patient placebo injections, to which he showed a dramatic response: He was able to give up his abnormal handwashing. Unfortunately, this turned out to be but a brief respite from his illness, for he resumed his ritual handwashing over the next few days.

At this point we began response prevention, turning off the tap in his room and limiting him to two minutes in the shower each day. Interestingly, he showed no nervousness during the ten-day period during which his handwashing was totally prevented. It was when the taps were turned on again that he briefly became anxious, for, as he put it, "when the taps were off I had no choice, so I could relax. It was when they were turned on again that I had to choose whether or not to wash again." Although his fear of infections continued to bother him, he did *not* increase his handwashing. We had removed the protective cocoon of compulsion, thus revealing the phobia, which now had to be dealt with by gradually exposing him to various feared objects and situations.

Other researchers have come to the same conclusions in the context of more extensive controlled studies: Exposure to the phobic situation reduces compulsive behavior slightly and much reduces the underlying fear. Response prevention dramatically reduces compulsive behavior, but only slightly helps the phobia. It is the combination of the two, response prevention followed by exposure to the feared situation, that works best.

Not all compulsions are as easy to prevent as handwashing. For the little girl who feared injuring others it was necessary to proceed somewhat differently. We taught her to dress more quickly by rewarding her for beating her previous record time for dressing. After a couple of weeks, she was dressing in a few minutes, the ritual having entirely disappeared. Then we proceeded to help her speed up other activities until she was able to drop all her rituals. But her fear that she might injure others persisted, a fear to which she could not be exposed. We therefore sent her to another hospital, where she could continue her education. After several months, her fear dissipated and she was able to return home. Her experience of living in a semi-protected environment had exposed her to various life situations in which the possibility of hurting others was present, so that her fear, no longer protected by the cocoon of her rituals, had gradually waned.

■

The most common form of exposure therapy in use today employs a graduated approach to the feared situation. This form of exposure is, of course, simpler to arrange for the more circumscribed phobias, such as fears of spiders or of thunderstorms, than for complex phobias such as the agoraphobia-panic syndrome. For the latter, practice must be carried out in situations that are less amenable to control than exposure to a spider. A shopping center may be more or less crowded, lines longer or shorter. But even in the case of the simple phobias, in order to conduct exposure therapy effectively, therapists must have a variety of props. These include videotapes and sound effects to treat fears of thunderstorms, buildings with outside stairways for the height phobic, and small rooms for the claustrophobic.

The first prerequisite is accurate diagnosis and a clear and detailed description of the phobia. To expose a person to the sights and sounds of thunderstorms is of no use if tornadoes are what he fears. Once the feared situation is well delineated, the therapist must arrange for practice within it. For a spider phobic, practice would mean putting a spider in a glass container, asking the patient first to approach the container—while the therapist provides encouragement and support—and then to put a gloved hand inside the container, and ultimately to let the spider run over the gloved fingers. When this no longer elicits fear, the same procedure is followed without the glove. When he reaches the point where he can hold the spider in his bare hand, the patient might be taken to places where spiders lurk and asked to search them out, thus ultimately exposing himself to all the cues that once elicited anxiety. For a spider phobic, this might take only three or four hours of exposure. For agoraphobia, however, perhaps fifty hours of exposure might be required to achieve an equivalent result. Indeed, in the case of the more complex phobias, patients need to be taught to become their own therapists and encouraged to continue self-administered practice until they feel entirely comfortable in their feared situations.

If the therapy for phobias is so simple, why haven't many more phobics discovered it, and cured themselves? In fact, some phobics do discover that exposure works, and go on to carry out a systematic program. However, we need to remember that all the forces are pushing the phobic in the opposite direction, toward more and more restriction of activity. The phobic feels so much relief when avoiding his phobic situation, that encountering it is the last thing he wants to do.

Exposure therapy, like so many medical procedures, is not painless. In one experiment designed to compare systematic desensitization, implosion therapy, and exposure, every patient experienced all of the three therapies. Asked which they preferred, eleven patients preferred desensitization, two preferred implosion, and only one preferred exposure. Yet ten of these patients considered exposure to be the most

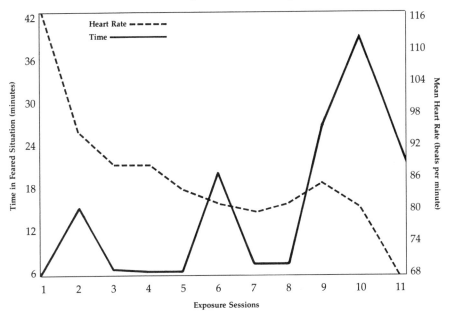

FIGURE 7-1

**Heart Rate Typically Decreases
as Feared Object Is Successfully Faced**

effective treatment. Thus, the therapist must warn patients that even though everything will be done to minimize discomfort, some anxiety is an inevitable accompaniment of the most effective therapy for phobia—exposure therapy.

◾

Despite the very real success of exposure therapy in the amelioration of fears, phobias, and the panic syndrome, a curious anomaly has been found to be associated with it. When someone is being successfully treated with exposure therapy, we would expect that a measure of fear, such as heart rate, would decrease as phobic avoidance decreases. This is the case with the phobic individual shown in Figure 7-1. As this patient's ability to look at a sharp knife (the feared object) increases, the heart rate decreases.

Another case, however, poses a more complicated picture. A young woman suffered from a phobia of what might be called "uncertainty." Whenever she feared that her husband might not be able to return from work at his usual hour, due to a delay of some kind, she became panic-stricken. Potential delays included the threat of bad weather,

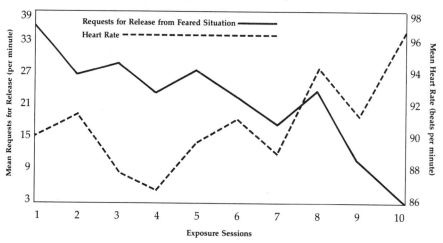

FIGURE 7-2

**A Less Typical Reaction: Heart Rate Increases
as Feared Object is Successfully Faced**

Requests for Release from Feared Situation ————
Heart Rate – – – – –

Mean Requests for Release (per minute)

Mean Heart Rate (beats per minute)

Exposure Sessions

and since she lived in northern Vermont, bad weather occurred frequently. This phobic anxiety, a variant of the panic syndrome, had
become so intense that she had lost nearly forty pounds in a few
months' time. The precipitating circumstance for her phobia was quite
clear: She and her husband were on their honeymoon in the north-
eastern corner of Vermont, a beautiful but lonely spot. One evening
he was fishing, and, caught up in the pursuit of his quarry, had moved
along the bank, away from his new wife. Suddenly she realized that
it was dark and that she was absolutely alone. She panicked. When
her husband found her she was shaking with fright and in tears. Not
surprisingly, this young woman had been raised in a very close family;
she could hardly remember an occasion on which she had been alone—
a case of pure separation anxiety in an adult.

To replicate this phobia in the laboratory for the purpose of accurate
measurement, we devised a situation of uncertainty. The patient was
asked to sit in a small room equipped with a foot pedal and was told
that the door would automatically lock when she entered the room,
and that she would have to press the pedal to open it. However, she
would not know on any one occasion whether one press or one thousand presses would be needed to unlock the door. This uncertainty
proved very frightening to her. As her treatment progressed and as
she improved, she was able to press the lever less rapidly, signaling
less need to escape from the feared situation. Her heart rate, however,

behaved in the opposite fashion; it increased as her avoidance decreased (see Figure 7-2). Despite this, she declared herself well and was able to function at home without apparent symptoms, even though she was physiologically aroused.

This discrepancy between behavior and physiological activity in the fear response has been called "desynchrony" and is found in some, but not all, phobics. From a therapeutic viewpoint, residual physiological discomfort is not desirable, and might even lead to a return of the original problem. Could pharmacological therapy, aimed at reducing physiological arousal, be helpful in such cases?

While exposure therapy has been used successfully, it is not completely effective. Although the follow-up studies described earlier demonstrated that patients were able to live much fuller lives as a result of treatment, few had entirely recovered. Results of exposure therapy, although a marked improvement over the previous therapies, fell short of the ideal. More work was needed to help perfect this promising therapeutic approach. The results of some of this work, including the role of pharmacological therapy in the treatment of phobia, will be examined in the next two chapters.

THE QUEST FOR A CURE: DRUG THERAPY 8

The theory of fears and phobias developed earlier in this book suggests that the secret of phobias in general, and of the panic syndrome in particular, lies in part in a faulty biological control mechanism, and that this mechanism may be modified, not only by learning, but by drugs. The notion that anxiety can be controlled by the use of drugs is not new. This is, after all, the age not only of anxiety, but also of the tranquilizer. In the context of phobia, however, psychological theories and approaches to treatment were dominant during the first half of this century, and the biological viewpoint was neglected. The prevailing opinion was that the neuroses, of which phobia is an example, were psychogenic disorders, and that only the psychoses were of biological origin. This perception tended to shape the research enterprise. To go against the grain of current opinion requires not only a new vision but also persistence, since the world of science is inherently conservative and may neglect the new and different.

■

Donald Klein, a psychiatrist working at the New York State Psychiatric Institute in the 1960s, noticed during the course of treating his patients that when agoraphobics panicked, they sought help from the nursing staff: "Patients ran to the nursing station . . . proclaiming that they were about to die. . . ." The nurses would comfort them and after about twenty minutes the patients would be able to leave, "their acute, overwhelming distress somewhat alleviated."[13] This behavior was reminiscent of the school-phobic child, who runs away from school to seek the comfort of home and parents. Dr. Klein began to suspect that adult panic reactions were a carry-over from the separation anxiety of childhood, a fear that, as we have seen, is a biologically endowed protective mechanism—in this case a protective mechanism that has gone wrong. Klein became convinced that these spontaneous panic attacks, or internal earthquakes, signaled the perturbations of a faulty biological control mechanism. If this were true, then agoraphobia could be viewed in a new way.

The nature of the *spontaneous* panic attack, as distinct from panic *caused* by being in a feared situation, remains an important missing link in our understanding of the genesis of the avoidance behavior characterizing agoraphobia. Because unexpected and unpredictable panic attacks always precede the onset of agoraphobia, it seemed likely to Klein that the panic attacks were causing the phobia. While Watson's little Albert learned to fear a harmless laboratory rat by associating a loud noise with the sight of the rat, such coincidences rarely occur in the real world. We have seen that learning by association can cause a phobia, but that such a cause is the exception rather than the rule. Could it be that the panic attack, set off by an oversensitive internal alarm system, functions in the same manner as Watson's loud noise, conditioning fear to the locations or situations in which panic attacks have occurred? Since rapid conditioning might be expected under such circumstances (little Albert learned his fear very quickly), then re-entering the situation, or even thinking about it, might in turn cause premonitory signs of panic, if not a full-blown attack. The agoraphobic who has suffered repeated conditioning has reason to retreat to the safety of home and family; separation fear has been reactivated.

This avoidance is also the cause of much of the misery and debilitation suffered by both the school-phobic child and the agoraphobic adult. In the case of children, not only is academic development compromised, but also social development—the ability to enjoy the companionship of other children, childhood games, and all the learning that derives from social intercourse. The adult, as we have seen, is similarly handicapped. Not only is life ultimately restricted to the confines of home, but so many simple things—even a pleasant walk—are fraught with anxiety and regarded with apprehension lest a panic attack occur.

All this would have remained but an interesting theory were it not for another observation by Klein, which was to have more practical ramifications. In the course of testing a number of what were at the time relatively new drugs under varying conditions, he made the discovery that imipramine—a drug that was the first effective anti-depressant to be discovered—seemed to block panic attacks. At the time, this was a serendipitous and somewhat startling finding, for imipramine was not thought to possess anti-anxiety qualities. Today, with the close connections between panic and depression becoming ever more apparent, it seems less of a surprise. This finding led Klein and his colleagues to conduct a series of experiments over the next twenty-five years to confirm the effectiveness of imipramine in the treatment of the panic syndrome.

■

Before describing these experiments, we need to review the methods by means of which the effectiveness of a new drug is assessed, as well as some of the stumbling blocks likely to be encountered along the way. To protect the patient, all new medical treatments should be carefully tested before being widely used. With all treatments there are pros and cons. Drugs often have troublesome side effects, and long-term problems may be discovered only after many years of use. Thus it is important to accurately delineate the positive effects of a medication. To do this, as we saw in the case of exposure therapy, controlled clinical trials are necessary. Trials of a new pharmacological agent have one major advantage over the testing of a new psychological therapy: The effects of the active drug can be compared with the effects of a placebo, a pill containing no active ingredient.

The "placebo effect" is still quite puzzling in its own right. The effects of almost every active medication can be mimicked in part by the administration of an inert substance, but only if patients *believe* that they are receiving the active drug and if they believe they will improve. One of the more astonishing findings of recent biological research is that the placebo effect, thought for many years to be entirely psychological in its mechanism, is in fact produced, at least in the instance of pain control, by prompting the secretion of pain-relieving substances. Here again we find an intricate interaction between psychological events and a chemical response within the brain.

This placebo effect is dramatically illustrated by the following true story: The introduction of the major tranquilizers prompted one research psychiatrist to carry out a controlled trial of their effectiveness with schizophrenic patients. As he was leaving for a summer vacation, he gave the resident medical staff a month's supply of the medication to be administered in accordance with his instructions, so that they could gain experience with its effects. When he returned from vacation, he was greeted with an enthusiastic report of the new drug. The staff reported that patients who had sat around the ward for years were now markedly improved; some hopeless cases had improved sufficiently to be discharged. To his—and their—amazement, he found that he had accidentally supplied the house staff with the placebo instead of the active medication, and that it was to the placebo that these remarkable results were to be credited! It is to control for these mysterious effects that the "double blind study" is used, that is, a study in which neither patient nor physician knows whether the active drug or a placebo is being administered.

To ensure against the bias that this knowledge might create in the physician or patient, pharmacological studies are arranged so that patients have an equal chance of being prescribed either the active drug or the placebo. The medications in the study are identical in appearance and, in ideal circumstances, have the same side effects.

A "single blind study" is a study in which the physician knows what the patient is receiving but the patient does not. This arrangement is often used early in the testing of a new medication, when the exact effects of the medication, or its dosage, have not been well established. Since the physician knows what the patient is getting, he can better adjust dosage or assess unusual effects. There are, however, sources of bias in such a study. For example, the physician may by his behavior give the patients clues as to which medication they are taking. To guard against this effect, the double blind study is used.

■

As we have seen, Klein considered the panic attack to be a manifestation of separation anxiety. Having found, in his uncontrolled studies, that imipramine seemed to block adult panic, he turned for his first controlled study to the childhood manifestation of separation anxiety, school phobia. Could childhood separation anxiety be contained by a medication? To test this question, school-phobic children were allocated at random to receive either a placebo or the active medication, imipramine. Neither the children nor their parents, nor the physician prescribing the medication, knew who was receiving the active medication and who the placebo.

This uncertainty on the part of both patient and physician as to whether or not the active medication is prescribed may reduce the effectiveness of the medication being tested in the clinical trial. Such a trial is not a perfect mirror of the clinical situation, for it minimizes the psychological components of belief and expectation that are better enhanced when both patient and physician believe in the treatment; rather, it is a conservative approach to treatment evaluation. Nonetheless, the randomized clinical trial is the acid test that must be applied to all new treatments, tempering the enthusiasm of its proponents with the realities of science.

In this instance, medication (active or placebo) was augmented by counseling the children and their parents on the need to return to school. By the end of the study, nearly twice the number of children treated with the active medication had returned to school as had those who received the placebo. Apparently the drug was markedly reducing the separation anxiety that had led to school phobia.

The results of this study were later reinforced by another experiment, this time using an animal model of separation. Rhesus monkeys make ideal subjects for such an experiment. They live in social groups and have a close relationship with their mothers for the first few months of life. At first the young are totally dependent; they expand their range of activities only slowly, and usually keeping mother in sight. Enforced separation during this period leads to a number of abnormal behaviors, including an inhibition of their normal exploration of the environment, which we might construe as analogous to school phobia. When young monkeys were, like the school children, given either imipramine or a placebo and then separated from their mothers, those receiving imipramine showed a much stronger tendency to explore on their own than those receiving the placebo—further evidence that the drug has a specific effect upon separation anxiety.

■

Having demonstrated that imipramine controlled the separation anxiety of the school phobic, Klein and his colleagues turned their attention once again to the adult variant of this disorder, the agoraphobia-panic syndrome. In a most compelling study, these physicians tested the theory that imipramine works by suppressing panic attacks. Patients with simple phobias, such as a fear of dogs or of heights, do not have panic attacks, so Klein reasoned that such phobics should show no benefit from imipramine. On the other hand, patients with the agoraphobia-panic syndrome should benefit. Both simple phobics and agoraphobics with panic were randomly allocated to receive either imipramine or a placebo. The results supported the theory nicely. Not only was no effect discernible in the case of the simple phobics, but those with the agoraphobia-panic syndrome who were given imipramine had fewer panic attacks and generally did much better than those given a placebo. The benefits of pharmacological treatment were both substantial and lasting in the majority of cases; two years after therapy had begun, only a quarter of those still taking the active medication had relapsed.

What takes but a moment to read took many years to accomplish. This explains why so few long-term controlled studies are undertaken: They are time-consuming and expensive. Preparatory studies—often short-term controlled studies—have to be completed before beginning the larger and more expensive effort; a sufficient number of patients have to be recruited; careful measurements must be carried out; the patients have to be treated; and their progress reassessed frequently. It takes a long time for a new treatment to be transformed into the reality of clinical practice, but such studies are the ultimate criterion upon which medical practice should be based. The patient should view with some suspicion any treatment, new or old, that has not undergone such testing. It is in the patient's interest to ask the physician for information about the testing history of any recommended treatment.

■

Another line of evidence added weight to Klein's finding that imipramine blocks panic. About twenty years ago it was observed that the infusion of sodium lactate into the bloodstream produced panic in patients with the disorder, but not in normal persons. Like many findings in science, this observation occasioned only mild interest at the time, since the study of panic was not yet in vogue. More recently, though, the ability to provoke panic attacks in the laboratory makes it possible not only to closely observe the phenomenon of panic but also to test the effect of imipramine in another way. Patients who suffer panic attacks following a lactate infusion are treated with imipramine and are then given another infusion of lactate. This time—following treatment with imipramine—panic attacks are much less likely to occur.

Recent work at Stanford suggests that the differences between normals and patients in their response to lactate have been exaggerated. From the very beginning of the experiment, even when they were resting quietly, the panic patients had a much higher heart rate than the normals. This was not unexpected; an intravenous infusion is likely to be more frightening to phobics than to normal controls. But the finding that the *proportional increase* in reported anxiety and in heart rate during the infusion of lactate was exactly the same for the normals as for the patients was not expected. The patients reached higher levels because they were more anxious to begin with. This is an important clue: It shows that a person already at a higher than normal level of anxiety is more likely to develop a panic attack. This is precisely what many patients report: When they enter their feared situation, they become increasingly anxious and then a panic attack begins.

Imipramine may work because it reduces the general level of anxiety, and thus reduces the likelihood of a panic attack.

■

Since compulsions are an elaboration of phobic avoidance, particularly in those individuals fearing either infection or the possibility of harming others, it seems reasonable to suppose that antidepressants might be useful in the treatment of this severe disorder. As is the case with agoraphobics, many victims of compulsive disorders are also depressed, and many also experience panic; medication might be beneficial either by reducing their anxiety or panic, or by relieving their depression.

Because compulsive ritualizing is much rarer than the panic syndrome, even most large centers will treat only a handful of such patients each year and few will have enough patients to complete a clinical trial. A number of pharmacological trials have therefore resulted in ambiguous findings. The few adequate studies we have suggest that clomipramine, an antidepressant related to imipramine, is the most useful drug in the treatment of compulsions. It is by no means clear whether the medication works by reducing depression—most of the evidence would suggest that it does—or by a more specific effect on compulsive ritualizing. There is, however, wide agreement that medication adds relatively little to treatment, as it reduces compulsive behavior only slightly.[14]

■

If imipramine is effective in reducing panic attacks and agoraphobic avoidance behavior, surely there is no need for exposure therapy! Since drug therapy is simpler—and perhaps even less costly, when a therapist's time is taken into account—then drug therapy should be the treatment of choice. The question arises, Can exposure therapy that teaches useful behavior be replaced by a drug? Can the same feelings of mastery and independence engendered by exposure therapy be acquired through drug therapy?

In fact, such a choice may be premature. If, as we saw in the last chapter, the amount of exposure is the major factor influencing the successful outcome of treatment, then any therapy will work only to the extent that it promotes exposure. Certainly this appears to be the case for psychological therapies. Now we must ask, Could it also be the case for pharmacological therapies? Could the effects observed in studies of these therapies be at least in part the result of exposure?

In all studies reporting the effective use of medication for the treatment of panic, patients have also been instructed to practice some form of exposure. To isolate the effects of drugs from the effects of exposure, a special type of control condition has to be established. The medication must be administered with instructions to patients *not* to expose themselves to their phobic situations. Such a design, because it inhibits patients from practicing exposure, obviously makes it impossible to examine fairly the degree of improvement in facing the feared situation. However, other indicators of improvement, such as a lowering of anxiety and panic, can be accurately observed.

To pursue this important question, a preliminary study was conducted in 1983 in our clinic at Stanford. Thirty-seven patients, all suffering from agoraphobia with frequent panic attacks, were randomly divided into three groups. One group received exposure therapy and imipramine; another received exposure therapy and a placebo; and the last received imipramine but was instructed to allow the medication time to work before venturing into the feared situation. They were thus discouraged from exposing themselves to the phobic situation. Neither the therapists nor the patients knew who was receiving the active medication and who the placebo, except for the last group, who knew they were receiving medication.

The first evaluation was done eight weeks after treatment began. Participants receiving imipramine showed marked improvement in depressive symptoms and a reduction in anticipatory anxiety, while those receiving the placebo showed no such improvement. None of the three groups showed a significant reduction in panic attacks. We

had shown that imipramine, in the absence of exposure, would reduce anticipatory anxiety and depression, but not panic.

At the next assessment, twenty-six weeks after treatment began, a clear finding emerged. Only the group receiving both exposure treatment and imipramine showed a reduction in panic attacks. Neither the drug alone, nor exposure alone, reduced panic. These findings suggest that the best treatment for the agoraphobia-panic syndrome is a combination of drug and exposure therapies. Each enhances the other. The drug, by reducing anticipatory anxiety, allows patients to expose themselves to the feared situation with less difficulty. But in the absence of systematic exposure to the feared situation, the drug's effects upon panic are nullified. Both the chemical effects and the effects of learning are needed to reduce panic.

One inescapable conclusion to be drawn from these studies is that combining the two therapies—exposure and drug—will be of greater help to the patient than either therapy alone. This conclusion is, however, only true for those with the agoraphobia-panic syndrome. For simple phobias, pharmacological agents contribute no additional benefit. Exposure alone is sufficient. For those patients who are in the early stages of the disorder and who have experienced only panic attacks, exposure therapy will add nothing to treatment, presumably because the patients are not avoiding anything. Drugs alone will suffice.

■

Given the remarkable finding that benzodiazepine receptor sites are found in the human brain, and that such receptor sites are part of a system modulating the fear response and perhaps panic, we might ask why the anti-panic effects of the benzodiazepines have not been more vigorously investigated. The answer is that these receptor sites have only recently been identified, and also that interest in the effect of the benzodiazepines upon panic has strengthened only in the last three or four years. Previously, the clinical impression had been that panic patients did not get better when treated with a benzodiazepine, so that while these compounds were widely used to treat mild anxiety, they were not used for panic. The neglect of these drugs in the treatment of panic and the absence of a controlled trial may be another example of the fads and fashions of therapeutics.

Recently, however, the results of a controlled study suggested that a benzodiazepine was surprisingly effective, at least in the short term, in suppressing panic. Now a newer benzodiazepine has been discovered that seems to have both antidepressant and anti-anxiety effects, much like imipramine. The efficacy of this drug, *alprazolam*, has been investigated in a double blind study. The results suggest that alprazolam is as effective as imipramine in controlling anxiety and panic, although it does not improve depressive symptoms to quite the same extent as imipramine. In an attempt to delineate the effects of alprazolam on panic, a number of controlled studies are now being carried out in the U.S. and in other countries. All this is good news for those suffering from the panic syndrome; an alternative pharmacological treatment would be especially welcome to those unable to tolerate the side effects of imipramine.

■

"Take this medication" is a deceptively simple instruction. Many people, perhaps half of those who try, miss doses, and some give up entirely. What appears to be easy turns out to be complicated. Human memory is fallible, and motivation (even to take a pill) is not always at the highest if one is tired, busy at other things, or in a situation where it would be embarrassing to take a pill. More importantly, medication tends to have side effects that, for some individuals, can be troublesome enough to discourage its regular use.

A few patients are so exquisitely sensitive to imipramine that they experience severe side effects at a very low dosage. Side effects probably account for the fact that about 20 percent of agoraphobic and panic patients drop out of controlled studies of imipramine—a rate double that for exposure therapy. The majority of patients can, however, tolerate the side effects of imipramine and the less severe side effects, such as dry mouth and stuffy nose, can be used as an index that a satisfactory level of the medication is being maintained in the body.

Another unresolved question is whether medication can be withdrawn without leading to a reappearance of symptoms. In short-term studies of a few weeks' or months' duration, participants experienced relapse as the drug was withdrawn. (Whether or not the medication can be withdrawn safely after longer use is unclear at present, as no study has attempted to answer this question.) This may strengthen the case for combining drug and exposure therapy. Exposure therapy, with its accompanying learning of new and more adaptive behaviors, may produce a stronger resistance to relapse—a hypothesis that must be more extensively explored in future research.

So far we have approached treatment on an individual basis, as if patients had no other relationships in life than those with a therapist or physician. Most people are not alone in this world, and the support of others—neighbors, friends, or relatives—may have important therapeutic implications. This theme will be explored in the next chapter.

SUPPORT FOR THE SUFFERER 9

It is the rare therapy that does not carry with it some discomfort for the patient—from the emotionally disturbing effects of the revelations that accompany psychotherapy to the sometimes harsh physical effects of surgery or of drugs. All successful therapy depends upon the patient's ability to stick with the treatment despite the inconveniences, the fear, and the pain. At the start of therapy physicians and patients often minimize the extent of the commitment required, with the result that the rough spots in treatment, especially if they are unexpected, may prove too much for some patients to endure. Exposure therapy is no exception. As we saw in an earlier chapter, patients find exposure to their feared situation to be an uncomfortable and at times scary experience. Yet they are asked to persist in their efforts, to make a continuing commitment to carry on in the face of discomfort ranging from a mild twinge of anxiety to excruciating fear.

A similar, if less crucial, challenge faces the person who decides to exercise to improve his or her health. No matter how good for one exercise may be, to get up early on a dark morning to run around the block and to pay for its benefits in the accompanying aches and pains may prove too much for all but the most hardy. It is the small daily decision that can be so difficult to make. For each of us, from the jogger to the phobic engaged in exposure therapy, the temptation is to stay at home and not face the discomfort or fear once again. There may, however, be ways to diminish the discomfort of exposure therapy and thus reduce the number of people who quit before they have received the maximum benefit.

It would seem obvious that the best way to expose patients to their feared situations is to do it gradually—and so avoid excessive anxiety—and at the same time to provide the support of a spouse or friend willing to help with the difficult task of exposure practice. Such a supportive relationship serves to extend the benefits of therapy over months and years instead of weeks, longer than is usually possible with a therapist. It may also reduce dependence upon the therapist and stimulate the patient's initiative.

What data have we gathered to indicate that this line of reasoning is correct? The first clue to what might be done to strengthen the patient's resolve came from a study in group therapy. The patients in the group under study had formed unusually close supportive relationships among themselves. This closeness inspired them not only to meet on their own between therapy sessions but to continue to meet even after therapy had been terminated. The purpose of their meetings was to encourage each other to continue exposure to their feared situations. The dropout rate for this closely knit group was much lower than that for patients treated either individually or in groups that did not foster such close relationships. Another clue came from reports of cases in which the spouses of agoraphobics had been included as co-therapists in a group treatment program. Again the dropout rate was low, and there was an additional benefit: The patients treated in this way maintained their gains longer than those treated by the therapist alone.

Also, when patients from the same neighborhood were grouped together for treatment, they showed more improvement than those in the more typical groups, in which the patients are drawn from different neighborhoods. Again the explanation was that neighbors, because of their accessibility to each other, continued to provide and receive mutual support and encouragement in facing their fears.

Three factors may be operating here. First, the support and encouragement of others motivates patients to reaffirm the daily decision to expose themselves to their feared situations. Second, the encouragement to practice exposure outside of therapy leads to more exposure to the feared situation than usually occurs when treatment is conducted solely by a therapist. (As we saw earlier, the decisive factor in therapy is the amount of exposure.) Third, because of the enhanced opportunities for practice, and the fact that they are more in control of their own therapy, patients can proceed at their own pace rather than at a pace set by a therapist. Confirmation of the influence of these factors comes from data revealing that intensive exposure carried out solely by a therapist results in dropout rates much higher than the dropout rates for treatment that includes some form of supportive relationship and practice outside of formal therapy.

These observations were first derived from *uncontrolled* studies, and, as we have seen, such studies, while suggestive, do not provide definitive evidence that one approach to treatment is better than another. They have recently been confirmed, however, by a *controlled* study that examined the effects of including spouses as co-therapists in the treatment of patients with agoraphobia accompanied by panic. All the patients were women and all had husbands who were willing to take part in treatment. Such selection factors may of course bias the outcome of an experiment; perhaps the very fact that a woman has a cooperative husband indicates that she possesses characteristics that would ensure a better outcome than usual. To control for subtle bias of this kind is difficult; those volunteering for a study might, for example, be different personality types from those who would refuse to be subjects for research. We cannot therefore generalize the results from any one study too widely; but given the initial clues about the importance of personal support in treating the agoraphobic, this controlled study was an important next step.

Twenty-nine couples were randomly allocated either to group therapy in which spouses were involved, or to group therapy without the presence of the husbands. In both groups, a graduated exposure therapy program was used; the women were encouraged to face their feared situations in a slow stepwise progression and at their own pace. In the spouse group, husbands were taught how to help their wives to face their feared situations. Of the twenty-nine agoraphobics only one dropped out of treatment, and that one was from the group assisted by husbands—a dropout rate of less than 4 percent. This finding suggested that it is graduated exposure, and not the spouses' presence, that leads to low dropout rates; the less frightening therapy can be made, the more effective it is. Moreover, the groups did not differ in their initial response to therapy. Such responses are calculated by averaging the progress made by each patient, and averages can be misleading, particularly in clinical trials. Suppose, for example, that out of ten people receiving treatment, eight showed no improvement and two showed 100 percent improvement. The average improvement would be 20 percent; yet no one actually improved 20 percent. In this instance the average would not reflect reality too well.

For a more precise estimate, the investigators established standards to determine the number of individuals in each group who were much improved as a result of therapy: 86 percent of those in the husband-assisted group had responded to therapy, as compared with less than 60 percent of those in the other group. This is a statistically significant difference. The enhanced responsiveness of agoraphobics to therapy facilitated by cooperative husbands is a definite advance. If such results were to be obtained more routinely, then we would expect to find that out of every 100 patients treated, eighty-two would gain significant benefit; this high degree of success reflects both the low dropout rates associated with graduated exposure and the enhanced outcome resulting from the participation of spouses.

■

Important personal relationships not only may affect the outcome of treatment, but may influence the course of agoraphobia in quite another way. As we have already seen, it has been suspected for many years that this disorder may have its beginnings in an over-close relationship. In the case of school phobia, perhaps a precursor of the panic syndrome, we know that an anxious mother can aggravate the symptoms by showing her own fear of separation from her child. Similar behavior on the part of husbands or wives may have similar effects. Two major theories have been put forward to account for the relationship between the symptoms of one partner and the behavior of the other.

Systems theory. The first of these theories suggests that a family should be viewed as a system that, like many physiological systems, tends toward a balanced state. If something changes in one part of the system, the entire system is perturbed, and an offsetting change must occur in other areas to reestablish balance.

Such a theory suggests that a symptom such as agoraphobia would tend to be maintained so that other family members could remain unperturbed, fixed in their accustomed roles. Should an agoraphobic begin to improve, then one of several changes would be set in motion: Adaptive behavior might occur on the part of other family members; another family member might develop symptoms; or failing such adjustments, the marriage might break up.

Early clinical observations suggested that the husbands of agoraphobics might themselves have neurotic symptoms. One study even suggested that such husbands had phobic symptoms similar to those of their wives but that the wives' symptoms were viewed as worse. If the wife's symptoms were removed, her husband would have to face his own illness openly; to avoid this, the family would foster the wife's symptoms. Larger-scale studies, using normal families as a control group, do not, however, find any evidence to support this notion. The spouses of agoraphobics are no more neurotic than are the spouses of nonagoraphobics.

The systems theory of phobia would also suggest that poor marriages might break up if the agoraphobic improves. In such marriages, the spouse does not have the capacity, or is insufficiently motivated, to make the necessary changes to adapt to the agoraphobic's improvement. The newfound independence of an improving agoraphobic calls for corresponding changes in the spouse—for example, giving up control of a number of areas that foster dependence, such as marketing, planning trips, or making critical decisions. The inability to make the necessary behavior changes would lead to increasing friction in the marriage, which might well lead to a stalemate; either the agoraphobic would be prevented from improving, or the marriage would break up because of the increased and unresolvable friction. Agoraphobics with a poor marital relationship would, then, be expected to do less well than agoraphobics with a good marital relationship.

Both clinical observation and well-controlled studies offer quite strong evidence for this hypothesis. One case report describes an agoraphobic woman whose symptoms disappeared when she left her husband, reappeared when she went back to him, and disappeared completely when she left him for good. Another report describes unusual jealousy on the part of the husband of an agoraphobic woman. As the wife's symptoms improved, the husband became increasingly suspicious of her newly acquired freedom: Was she seeing someone else? As improvement continued, these suspicions grew, and outbursts of accusation and anger became frequent. Ultimately, these outbursts led to deterioration on the wife's part, and she once more became housebound. The marital balance had been restored.

While these clinical observations are suggestive, a better test of this hypothesis—that patients in a poor marital relationship do not do as well as those in a good marital relationship—is to measure the degree of marital satisfaction before therapy begins. The results of two inquiries prove most interesting: Immediately following treatment, there were no differences in the degree to which symptoms had improved. But six months later, those with the poorer marriages tended to relapse, while those with more satisfactory marriages did not. The husbands in the poorer marriages could not adapt to their spouses' improvement; the only way to maintain the stability of the marriage was for the symptomatic spouse to hang on to her symptoms.

Reinforcement theory. Skinnerian theory would suggest a different view of the agoraphobic marriage, a view not incompatible with the systems theory of homeostasis but with a different emphasis. The theory of natural selection states that species that adapt to their environment will tend to be preserved. Similarly, behaviors that benefit the organism are maintained, while those that result in harm are not. Skinner has demonstrated that behavior is sensitive to its effects upon the environment. If we believe, as Skinner does, that the social environment is responsible for the development and maintenance of many symptoms, then the spouse's behavior, as a factor in the environment, must influence the agoraphobic's symptoms. Well-intended behavior, for example, could have unintended deleterious effects. Following the first few panic attacks, a husband might, out of solicitude, temporarily take over some of his wife's tasks—shopping for groceries would be an obvious necessity. As the panic attacks continued, the temporary might become permanent. The husband would reinforce his wife's disability by not expecting her to show independent behavior. The persistence of such oversolicitous behavior during a treatment program might well retard the wife's recovery.

■

Both theories—the family systems theory and Skinnerian theory— suggest that marriage counseling might prove useful in the treatment of agoraphobia. We know from one controlled study that marital therapy cannot replace exposure therapy. In this study, one group of phobic patients was randomly allocated to marital therapy, another group to exposure therapy. Those in the marriage therapy group showed an improved marital relationship, but no improvement in their phobias. Those in exposure therapy showed the expected improvement of their phobias, and, as a consequence, an improvement in their marital relationship. Once again we see that exposure to the feared situation is absolutely necessary to improve phobic behavior. Thus, the function of marital therapy would seem to be as an addition to exposure therapy.

To test the theories concerning marriages in which one partner has a behavioral disability, and at the same time to test the practicality of adding a form of marital therapy to exposure therapy, we recently completed a study of twenty-five couples. In each of these one of the partners had agoraphobia with panic attacks. In addition to the usual objective measurement of phobic behavior taken before the beginning of treatment, an assessment of marital communication was made by videotaping each couple while they tried to resolve a problem of mutual concern. These videotapes were scored for positive and negative communications by observers who knew nothing of the purpose of the study.

The first steps in the study were to treat all the agoraphobics with therapist-supervised exposure carried out in small groups, and to conduct meetings in which the couples learned how to proceed with home practice. A manual outlining the tasks and responsibilities of each partner was provided for both the patient and spouse. This treatment approach produced the expected low dropout rate; only one couple discontinued treatment. Following treatment and measurements aimed at determining the amount of improvement, the experiment proper began. Patients were paired on the basis of their degree of improvement, and one of each paired couple was allocated by chance selection to one of two treatment groups. One group was given communication skills training; the other was given relaxation training as a control procedure. In each group, spouses accompanied patients and participated in the training.

Communication skills training consisted of teaching several specific behaviors to be practiced by couples first in the therapeutic group and later at home. The first aim was to enhance the quality of communication by teaching each partner certain techniques—to pay accurate attention to what the other was saying, to phrase statements more accurately, to make constructive (rather than impossible) requests, to deliver constructive feedback to requests, and to seek clarification of statements. Naturally, communications tended to focus on the symptoms as they affected the marriage and to clarify what part the spouse could play in helping the agoraphobic partner. As treatment progressed, and the couple's communication skills improved, negotiating skills were taught. Each couple was helped to formulate a problem in an accurate and well-defined way, to generate a series of potential solutions, and then to devise and agree upon a concrete solution to the problem. Eight of these sessions completed the course.

In the post-treatment assessment to determine whether, and to what extent, this training had affected the couples' ability to handle problems, the couples were once more videotaped as they were attempting to solve a problem. For those who had had the benefit of communication skills training the amount of positive behavior was almost doubled and the amount of negative behavior halved, but those who had received only relaxation training showed no changes. In the light of the success of communication skills training, the next question became, Was there any effect on the phobia? The answer was quite clear: On all the measurements of agoraphobia, those in the communication skills group improved significantly more than those in the relaxation group. One exception to this was in the measure of panic; the relaxation training group appeared to do better on this score; however, those in this group also went out less frequently than the other group. When the measure of panic was adjusted for the amount of exposure to the phobic situation, the groups were exactly equal. We can conclude that communication skills training following exposure therapy results in continued gains for the agoraphobic. If no training follows exposure therapy, there is usually no further improvement, or even a slight decline.

Our study next attacked the theories of marital interaction more specifically. Would improvements in symptoms lead to deleterious changes in the marriage? This study provided no evidence for an affirmative answer. Nor did improvement lead to deterioration in the psychological functioning of the spouse. Some differences in the behavior patterns of the two treatment groups did emerge, however: Among those being trained in communication skills, the more frequently the agoraphobic was able to leave the house the greater was the marital satisfaction. The pattern in the others was just the opposite: The more the agoraphobic was able to get out, the worse the marriage fared. These data support the Skinnerian position on the reinforcement of symptoms. Those couples with better communication skills could better adapt to the symptom changes. In the group untrained in communication skills, improvement of symptoms apparently led to increased conflict, with spouses perhaps becoming resistant to changing their supportive behavior as the agoraphobic became more independent. Indeed, continued support for the phobic's effort to achieve greater independence occurred only in those receiving communication skills training. For the other group such support lessened after exposure therapy was completed.

Finally, did those with poorer marriages tend to do worse than those with good marriages? No. However, it should be noted that few couples with problem marriages were to be found amongst the agoraphobics in this study.

The support of a spouse or a friend undoubtedly helps the agoraphobic to better negotiate the difficult path to greater freedom, particularly if the focus of support is to encourage exposure practice. Such a supportive relationship leads to a much reduced dropout rate from therapy. Even more can be accomplished, it seems, by teaching marital partners some simple communication skills that help to alleviate the stresses imposed upon the marriage by the agoraphobic's increasing independence, and to smooth the problems that so often occur during exposure practice. Not only should the focus be upon the whole patient, but also upon the whole environment of the patient, of which the family is one of the most important aspects.

FACING OUR FEARS 10

Reading this book may have piqued your interest about fears that you yourself experience. It can be interesting—and helpful—to take a closer look at those fears. If your fears cause little or no interference with your everyday life, they are common fears. If there is significant interference with everyday life, you may have a phobia. To help you decide, let's look at some of the more common phobias. If you are eager to assess your fears—and feel you have a sufficient grasp of the nature of these phobias, skip to page 120.

Animals. Probably a carry-over from a traumatic experience in childhood. Although the original incident may have been forgotten, later experiences may revive the accompanying emotions. The most common animal phobias are of dogs and cats. The need to avoid any place where one is likely to encounter so common an animal as a cat or dog obviously leads to a drastic limitation of mobility. This can be overcome to a considerable extent by planning—by using an automobile instead of walking, for example. But visits to the homes of friends who have cats or dogs as pets become impossible, and even pictures of the feared animal may cause significant anxiety. Dreams of being attacked by the animal are not uncommon, and the sight of the animal in the distance will lead to immediate avoidance—perhaps making a detour or turning back, hailing a cab or jumping on a bus. Like all phobias, this fear of the most commonly encountered animals demands a constant vigilance on the part of the sufferer.

Insects. Few people, aside from entomologists, actually like spiders, although not everyone actively fears them. The fear of insects and spiders usually falls within the realm of common fears, but may occasionally reach phobic proportions. As with any phobia, this one is marked by an avoidance of places where the feared objects are likely to be encountered—in the case of spiders, cellars and dark cupboards would be among the places avoided. The spider phobic may live in a protected environment well sprayed with insecticide, or policed by a friend or relative. Before retiring for the night, the phobic may fearfully search the room for the insect, probably well armed with a can of insecticide. Or, better still, someone else will search the bedroom and declare it safe. Nightmares about spiders are common, and the sight of one leads to immediate flight.

Heights. For the true acrophobic, even the thought of looking down from a high place will bring on a sensation of falling and dizziness. The view from a window high above the street, often a scenic view much admired by others, will lead to a chilling feeling of anxiety. It is the vertical view, and the accompanying anticipation of falling, that are the most frightening elements of this phobia. The acrophobic will assiduously avoid all high places and will frequently have anxiety-laden dreams of falling. The limitations of this person's social and business life are significant; he or she cannot attend meetings in certain buildings, spend a night in certain hotels, or go to parties in apartments that look out over the spectacular rooftops of Paris or New York. A fear of heights may be aggravated by an associated fear of injury. In some cases, the phobia is actually a fear of injury caused by falling. Flying may also pose a problem, although many height phobics are not troubled by airplane travel. The view from the insulated interior of an airplane is very different from the vertical unprotected view from an exposed high place.

Storms. Often a prolongation of a childhood fear, perhaps learned from a fearful parent, the fear of storms may be quite specific—it may be limited, for example, to tornadoes—or it may be all-inclusive. Thunder and lightning are common specific fears. The rumble of thunder or a flash of lightning may be the feared event, which generalizes to all sudden noises and flashes of light, or to all dark, cloudy days. The storm phobic's life is dominated by his view of the weather—and by the weather forecast. Anxiety mounts as the weatherman depicts a storm moving toward the area. Such a forecast may lead the phobic to stay at home that day or to leave work early in order to reach home in time to avoid the storm. An actual storm demands extreme avoidance: The drapes are closed, and the phobic retires to a cellar or a closet, where the sights and sounds of the storm will be attenuated.

Enclosed places. The compulsion to avoid all small enclosures or places where they may be trapped rules out for many claustrophobics even the barber's chair, let alone airplanes. This phobia is often accompanied by a fear of crowded places, as these enhance feelings of confinement and the fear of being trapped. Claustrophobics will avoid elevators, so that to reach a high floor in a building requires an exhausting climb, or is completely impossible. To diminish the feeling of entrapment, the claustrophobic may demand that the windows of small rooms at home be kept open, or even that the doors be removed. This phobia may also be accompanied by fears of suffocation or of choking.

Flying. This phobia may stem from other fear sources such as claustrophobia or acrophobia. When the door of the airplane is closed, the claustrophobic is faced with the terrifying thought of not being able to leave for a fixed period of time—perhaps several hours. The tubular space of the aircraft presses in, and the suffocating feeling of being trapped emerges. Most airplane phobics are afraid that the plane will fall apart and crash. Any indication that something is wrong—a slight jolt on takeoff, minor turbulence, strange noises—may cause intolerable anxiety. Many people with a phobic fear of flying will manage to get to the airport, only to balk at the last moment and return home. Many get to their destinations by automobile, bus, or train. The cost in time and opportunities for travel are obvious, as are the interference with both work and leisure.

School phobia. This disorder, which usually strikes during the early school years, may, as we have seen, be the precursor of the agoraphobia-panic syndrome, and is best conceptualized as separation anxiety. It is often engendered by an anxious, overprotective parent—by the nature of things, more often the mother than the father. Seen as avoidance of school, it is actually a reluctance to leave the protection of home, most commonly demonstrated at the beginning of the school year, of the semester, or even of the school week. Physical symptoms may play a dominant role in the disorder; characteristically, after a normal weekend a child will complain of feeling ill, of having a headache or stomachache, sometimes vomiting. An attempt to force the child to go to school may provoke panic. At school the child is distracted, cannot concentrate on tasks, and may leave without permission. Unlike the truant, the school phobic immediately returns home, the only place of comfort.

■

With the exception of school phobia, most of the phobias described above are not associated with panic attacks. Some of them, however, may sometimes be part of the more complex agoraphobia-panic syndrome.

Although we have spent much time examining this serious disorder—and the media have recently called attention to it—let us consider its main features once more: The first symptom is usually an unexpected panic attack. Many individuals will continue to have only panic attacks, never progressing to the full-blown disorder. Others will develop agoraphobia. Panic is a markedly physical feeling, rapid in onset, quickly building to a peak, and typically lasting for about twenty minutes. The attacks seem totally mysterious and may come out of the blue. Bodily feelings may center on the heart, with a rapid pulse and dull pain over the chest, along with fears of an impending heart attack. Or they may involve rapid breathing with a feeling of suffocation. Or there may be dizziness, coupled with feelings of unreality, and a feeling of great distance from the world, or of being outside one's body. Other symptoms include intestinal pain, sweating, hot and cold flashes, and a fear of dying, going crazy, or losing control. Several of these symptoms usually occur during a panic attack.

Such attacks may lead the sufferer to visit a succession of physicians in search of an explanation for the mysterious disorder, so that the syndrome acquires a hypochondriacal overtone. These attacks usually begin in late adolescence or in early adult life; they may follow a drug experience with LSD, marijuana, or cocaine. Other precipitating factors include illness, overwork, and loss of—or separation from—a person to whom one is strongly attached. The usual frequency of attacks is about three per week, although a single massive attack, perhaps followed by one or two smaller ones, and then a free spell for months or years is not uncommon. Others may experience several attacks a day. As time goes on, the likelihood of developing phobic limitations becomes stronger, as the circumstances in which the attacks occur multiply, conditioning fear to the increasing number of situations and places in which they have occurred.

The agoraphobic, like the school phobic, views home as a safe place. Usually there is difficulty in both walking and driving alone; trips are easier with a spouse, or with a close friend. Longer trips, such as vacations or business trips, may be almost impossible, or filled with

TABLE 10-1

Assessing Your Fears

Feared Objects, Situations	A Mild Discomfort	B Can Face It If I Must	C Avoid at All Costs
Accidents			
Airplanes			
Bats			
Being alone			
Being in a new place			
Birds			
Blood			
Boating			
Bridges			
Cats			
Cemeteries			
Crawling insects			
Criticism			
Crowded rooms			
Crowds			
Darkness			
Dead animals			
Dead bodies			
Death			
Deep water			
Dentists			
Dirt			
Dogs			
Driving an automobile			
Elevators			
Enclosed places			
Feeling disapproved of			
Feeling rejected			
Flying insects			
Guns			
Harmless snakes			
Heights			
Illness			
Injections			
Losing control			
Loud voices			
Meeting a stranger			
Mental illness			
People in authority			
Prospect of surgery			
Public speaking			
Rats and/or mice			
Sharp objects			
Sick people			
Sirens			
Spiders			
Sudden noises			
Suffocating			
Thunderstorms			
Trains or buses			
Walking alone			
Wounds			

dread. Always there is the fear—and indeed the chance—that a trip will precipitate a panic attack. Many subsidiary fears may be present, including fears of crowded places, restaurants, heights, elevators, and so on. This is one of the most generalized phobias, and the fear list is liable to be extensive. At the worst, the agoraphobic is essentially housebound; this is one of the most severe disabilities associated with a behavior disorder.

■

The questionnaire (see Table 10-1) may help you identify your fears and determine whether you have a normal fear, a phobia, or the panic syndrome.

Across from each fear are listed three possible degrees of discomfort elicited by the particular situation: *Mild discomfort* indicates exactly that—a mild feeling of tension in the presence of the feared object or situation. *Can face it if I must*, while requiring effort and control to master the discomfort, is not of a degree to cause total avoidance. The object can be viewed or the situation entered and endured if need be in the ordinary course of life. *Avoid at all costs* is the criterion of disabling fear; indeed, perhaps even thinking about the object or situation is anxiety-provoking; should you accidentally encounter it, your reaction would be to flee. If the item causes no discomfort, simply leave it blank.

Having completed all the questions, the next step is to look at your responses and, if there are a sufficient number, group them into patterns of fear. A flow chart will help you do this (see Figure 10-1). For example, a *fear of injury* might include these items: sharp objects, blood accidents, wounds, guns, the prospect of surgery—all aspects of a single fear. *Claustrophobia* might include suffocating, airplanes, enclosed places, crowded rooms, elevators. *Social fears* could include criticism, meeting a stranger, people in authority, public speaking, feeling rejected or disapproved of. *A fear of heights* might include airplanes, bridges, high places. *Separation fear* could include being alone, being in crowds, driving an automobile, death, walking alone, losing control.

If few of the items in a particular fear grouping are at the top level of intensity—*Avoid at all costs*—then it is likely that the fear causes little or no interference with your life. In this case you have a set of normal fears. If significant avoidance exists, and thus a great deal of interference with everyday life, you may have a simple phobia, ago-

FIGURE 10-1
Self-Assessment of Fears and Phobias

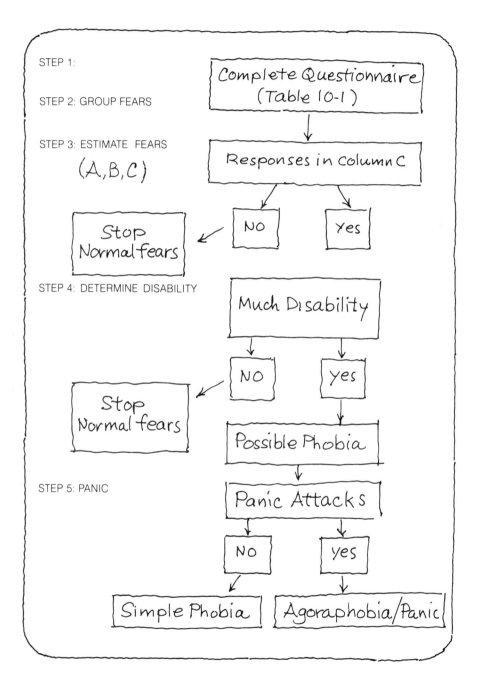

STEP 1:

STEP 2: GROUP FEARS

STEP 3: ESTIMATE FEARS

(A,B,C)

STEP 4: DETERMINE DISABILITY

STEP 5: PANIC

Complete Questionnaire (Table 10-1)

Responses in column C

NO   Yes

Stop Normal fears

Much Disability

NO   yes

Stop Normal fears

Possible Phobia

Panic Attacks

NO   yes

Simple Phobia   Agoraphobia/Panic

TABLE 10-2

Treatment for Fears, Phobias, and Panic

Children's Fear	Parent-assisted Exposure
Severe Fear Minor Simple Phobia	Self-exposure
Simple Phobia Complex Phobia	Therapist-assisted Exposure
Agoraphobia/Panic	Drug Therapy Therapist-assisted Exposure Spouse-assisted Exposure
Panic	Drug Therapy Self-exposure, If Needed

raphobia, or panic attacks without phobia. In that case, the next question to ask is whether the disability caused by the problem, either in the intensity of anxiety or the extent of avoidance, is enough of a handicap to require treatment.

■

Self-assessment is not a replacement for professional help. The intent of this chapter is in part to prepare you for a professional consultation, should you wish one, so that you will know what sort of questions to ask. Another aim is to highlight ways in which you can help yourself. The treatment alternatives for fears, phobias, and panic are shown in the table above. A quick glance indicates that the treatments range from parent-assisted or self-exposure to a combination of drug therapy and exposure, as we move from a severe common fear to the agoraphobia-panic syndrome. For the sake of clarity and further exposition, let us look at each of the different levels separately, highlighting special cases along the way.

Most children's fears are soon outgrown and do not need special attention. Some, however, may cause suffering or limitations that parents can help to ameliorate. The simplest way to deal with a child's fears is to design an exposure program and to help the child complete it. The basic principles of such a program are *gradualism* and *reward*. An exposure hierarchy should begin with what the child can do.

For example, if your child has a fear of the water but can visit a beach and perhaps play close to the water's edge, then that is where to begin. From there you can plan a series of graduated approaches to deeper water. You might sit on the beach, letting the water occasionally lap over your legs, perhaps playing a game with your child. With care the child will be able to tolerate splashes of water and may soon become comfortable sitting in shallow water. During each step of the process, praise should be given for progress and the depth of the water gradually increased, until the fear has vanished. To accomplish this might take one afternoon or several days, depending on the severity of the fear.

For fears of cats or dogs, consider exposing the child to kittens or puppies, and if the child takes to one, buy it. The slow growth of a puppy into a dog will allow the child gradual exposure to his fear. When the dog is grown, begin approaching strange dogs, small ones at first, and encourage the child to pet the animal. Again, give plenty of praise for progress.

Remember that most simple phobias begin in childhood. If it is possible—and we don't know that it is—to prevent the occurrence of phobias in adult life, then childhood is the time to begin. If fear and avoidance are dealt with early in life, phobias will be less likely to persist into adult life. For this reason, it may be particularly important to deal with separation fears adequately during childhood. The method used to diminish this class of fears is exactly the same as that described above. The child who is diffident about leaving home should be encouraged to do so; this may force the parents to face and overcome whatever irrational fears they have about the safety of the child. Again, the process should be gradual so as to steadily build the child's confidence that he can safely leave home.

∎

The most effective treatment for severe fears and simple phobias is exposure therapy, featuring the same principle of gradualism as that used in parent-assisted exposure. For most adults self-exposure should suffice, but should that prove ineffectual, then a therapist may be needed. As no drug therapy is involved, the program can be handled by a licensed clinical psychologist or counselor. Remember, though, that psychologists and counselors differ in their skills and interests. Many practice only psychotherapy, which has not proved an efficient way to treat phobias. So make sure that the therapist you choose is familiar with exposure therapy.

In the case of self-exposure, you may want to enlist the help of a spouse or friend, whose role is described below in the section on agoraphobia. First find out exactly how closely you can come to the feared situation without evoking more than mild anxiety. Then construct a plan by which you can slowly approach it. For example, in the case of a fear of elevators, you might at first be able to go up only one floor. Find a tall building, preferably with an uncrowded elevator that stops at every floor. Practice going up two floors until your anxiety is eliminated. Continue to add one floor at a time. Don't forget to generalize your gains by practicing in other buildings and in more crowded situations. Keeping a chart or a graph of your gains can strengthen motivation by providing tangible evidence of your progress. Remember that exposure is not painless. Overcoming the mild discomfort provoked by each additional step is essential to your progress. Sometimes one's fear levels vary, so that what is comfortable on one day may prove more anxiety-provoking the next. Do not be discouraged by this.

In some parts of the country there exist organized groups that help promote exposure to particular feared situations. The most common of these attacks the fear of flying. Often run by pilots in conjunction with a psychologist, such programs offer both education about flying and its safety and a gradual approach to flying itself, culminating in one or more flights. Again, it is important to remember that you must practice your newfound skills; unless you consciously sustain your gains, it is likely that the fear will return.

■

School phobia. One of the few childhood phobias to require treatment, this disorder is believed by many to be akin to the adult agoraphobia-panic syndrome. The key element in treatment is the cooperation of the parents to ensure attendance at school; this requires exposure to the feared situation, namely, separation from home. Teachers as well as parents may have to become involved in the therapeutic process. The exposure program can be handled by a psychologist, but because there is evidence that the drug imipramine is helpful in this disorder, psychiatric care may be needed.

Social phobia. Fear and avoidance of social situations tend, we know, to be common in adolescence and are usually overcome in the course of growing up as shyness recedes and social situations become enjoyable. For some people, however, the fear persists, ranging from avoidance of specific social situations to avoidance of almost any new relationship. Its elements may include a fear of authority figures, for example older persons, bosses, and so on; a fear of public speaking, that is, addressing an audience or participating in meetings; a fear of crowded rooms; or a fear of the opposite sex. In its most severe form this phobia may be accompanied by panic attacks.

The principles underlying the treatment of this condition are the same as for any phobia, namely exposure to the feared situations. The first task is to explore the dimensions of the phobia and to decide where practice should begin. The problem faced by the social phobic, however, is that social situations are not as accessible for practice or as controllable in their dimensions, as many other phobic objects or situations. Unless the feared situation is narrow and can be practiced easily, professional help will be needed.

A common theme underlying many of the social phobic's problems is a lack of assertiveness; such persons literally shy away from many human interactions, blushing, looking away rather than maintaining eye contact, slouching rather than standing squarely, and mumbling or whispering rather than talking clearly. All these behaviors are aspects of avoidance, the physical shrinking away from feared contacts; but they also complicate the problem, for others often respond to these behaviors by losing interest in the conversation, so that rejection adds to the plight of the social phobic.

Assertive behavior is a skill like any other and can be learned.[15] The elements include a firm gaze, better body posture, and a normal conversational voice. Practice of more assertive behavior, as with anything else, makes perfect; the new behavior can be tried out in many situations, beginning perhaps with a spouse and moving on to strangers and in increasingly difficult circumstances. The same behavior techniques apply to public speaking. There are always one or two people in the audience who will attend to the speaker, smiling and nodding encouragingly. By speaking directly to such people, the challenge is reduced from a speech to an audience to a talk to one or two strangers and is correspondingly easier to handle.

Assertive behavior can be taught by a skilled psychologist or counselor who can also help devise the various practice situations needed to overcome this problem. Social phobia may be accompanied by panic attacks, in which case medication will be needed in addition to psychological treatment; in these circumstances consultation with a psychiatrist may become necessary.

Compulsive disorder. As we have seen, the treatment of this serious disorder is divided into two parts—response prevention to remove the compulsions, followed by exposure therapy to treat the residual phobia. Treatment in an in-patient setting is often required, and if this is the case, a center specializing in the treatment of phobias and compulsions should be selected; an appropriate center will often be located within a teaching hospital affiliated with a medical school. Response prevention may be used continuously for several days, or alternatively may be limited to several hours a day, with the patient practicing restraint between sessions. In the latter case, a combination of response prevention and exposure to feared items may be used.

Family members are often caught up in the web of compulsive behavior and must accordingly be involved in the later stages of treatment. As treatment progresses, the family must learn to withdraw from participation in the patient's rituals—a task they should carry out under the direction of a skilled therapist. Whether treatment is being conducted on an in-patient or an out-patient basis, relatives must understand that response prevention can be extremely anxiety-provoking for the patient. To preserve home as a "safe place," the patient may try to make secret contracts with the family to leave unchanged a particular aspect of the compulsive ritual. This collusion would obviously reduce the effectiveness of response prevention by allowing the patient an escape route. The compulsive may also become angry with the treatment team for continuing response prevention and, in the hope of being rescued from the hospital or modifying the treatment plan, may devise other schemes, such as complaining of mistreatment to family members. It is important that such attempts to derail therapy should be discussed with the treatment team.

If depression accompanies compulsive behavior, as it so often does, drug therapy, using an antidepressant agent, may be necessary. If response prevention proves successful, the residual phobic symptoms will require treatment with exposure therapy. Again, the family may have to become involved in the treatment process by supporting the patient's home practice in confronting the phobic objects or situations.

The agoraphobia-panic syndrome. This most complex of the phobic disorders requires careful professional assessment and treatment by a psychiatrist. A psychiatrist experienced in using the most up-to-date treatment methods, namely a combination of exposure and drug therapies, should be selected.

Overcoming a complex problem such as agoraphobia demands persistence in the face of the difficulties and setbacks encountered during treatment. As we have seen, exposure to feared situations can be scary, and treatment with medication may result in unwelcome side effects. Successful treatment demands that the patient persist with exposure despite fear, and with medication despite its side effects. Usually both the fear and the side effects can be minimized, but in the early stages of treatment patience and fortitude are necessary. The most commonly used medications are the tricyclic antidepressant imipramine (Tofranil) or monoamine oxidase inhibitors (Nardil, Marplan); and the benzodiazepine, alprazolam (Xanax). Side effects from these medications are common, although it should be remembered that such effects are a sign that the drug is achieving therapeutic levels. The dosage needed may vary considerably among individuals: Some patients respond to low doses; others need high doses to obtain good effects.

Persons subject only to panic attacks can be managed entirely with medication. For the agoraphobic, exposure is absolutely essential—usually a combination of therapist-assisted exposure followed by spouse-assisted exposure. Because of their panic attacks, exposure treatment for agoraphobics is more complicated than for phobics.

As with simple phobia, it is essential for the agoraphobic to practice in the phobic situation every day, even though exposure may have to extend over months. A hierarchy of feared situations should be devised much as for simple phobia; however, because of the generalized nature of agoraphobia this task demands more complex planning. All the situations that have been avoided over the years should be listed, and the least fear-provoking should be the first attacked. A typical goal to be worked toward might be to shop alone in a supermarket. The first step might be to drive farther and farther from home, until the ride to the selected shopping center can be completed without anxiety. The same gradual approach should then be taken to entering the supermarket—at first parking in the lot, and, finally, entering the store and staying for increasing lengths of time—first at an hour when few people are there, then in more crowded situations, and, ultimately, making purchases and learning to tolerate the anxiety of standing in the checkout line. The aim should be to work gradually toward a completely normal response. Ups and downs should be expected; repeated practice in the same situation, until it becomes completely comfortable, is essential.

While practicing, it is a good idea to be aware of one's thoughts. Not surprisingly, they are often negative: "I can't do this, it will make me too scared," or "I'm sure I'll faint if I go on." Such thoughts should be challenged; they are not realistic, and they are defeatist. They should be replaced by positive thoughts, such as "This is getting easier to do; doing it makes me feel good." These deliberate efforts will help to further the aims of practice, and are a first step in overcoming the often rather negative mind set of the agoraphobic.

What most agoraphobics fear, of course, is a sudden attack of panic, although such attacks are rare during periods of practice. If an attack does occur it is important that it not end in flight. When panic strikes, the first thing to do is to backtrack a little from the place in which it happened. Try and find a nearby place to sit down for a while, so that you can relax and let the feeling dissipate. Confront scary thoughts such as "I must be having a heart attack," "I'm going to go crazy if this keeps up." These fears are unwarranted; such things do *not* happen during panic attacks. Instead, relax, and do not pay undue attention to your bodily feelings. They are merely the accompaniment of anxiety, and will dissipate in a few minutes. You are not in danger. When the attack is over, immediately confront the phobic situation. Once a panic attack passes it is unlikely to recur for a while; don't let it disrupt your practice.

As we have seen, a husband or wife (or a friend) can play an important part as an auxiliary therapist in the treatment of agoraphobia. The role of a spouse is twofold—first, to encourage greater independence on the part of the agoraphobic, and second, to help structure the practice sessions and motivate the patient. In both these roles it is essential for the spouse or friend not to be critical, but rather to encourage and to be unsparing of praise for achievement. The agoraphobic and the spouse should be able to communicate frankly and effectively. Any problem raised during the course of practice should be· identified as concretely as possible and a solution worked out.

As with any therapy, a record of the progress being made provides feedback, enhances motivation, and allows problems to be quickly identified. The agoraphobic should keep a diary of progress (see Table 10-3 for a sample record form). To assist with record-keeping is another role for the spouse. Progress can be more immediately evident by plotting graphs, using the data from the diary. A graph of progress toward the goal of spending sixty minutes in a shopping center is displayed in Figure 10-2. Note that there are ups and downs in the otherwise steady progress made by this patient. Setbacks often occur early in the practice sequence, but they will be less discouraging if

TABLE 10-3
Self-Monitoring Form

Date	Task	Accomplished	Notes
	GOAL BEHAVIOR (To spend 60 minutes in the shopping center)		
11/2	Drive to shopping center, stay in parking lot 10 minutes	yes	
11/2	Drive to shopping center, stay in parking lot 15 minutes	yes	
11/3	Drive to shopping center, stay in parking lot 15 minutes	yes	
11/3	Drive to shopping center, enter store, stay for 2 minutes	yes	
11/3	Drive to shopping center, enter store, stay for 5 minutes	yes	
11/5	Drive to shopping center, enter store, stay for 10 minutes	yes	
11/5	Drive to shopping center, enter store, buy one item	yes	felt a bit anxious.
11/6	Drive to shopping center, enter store, buy one item	yes	feels fine.

FIGURE 10-2

Daily Performance Recorded in Graph Form
Early Setbacks Are Successfully Overcome

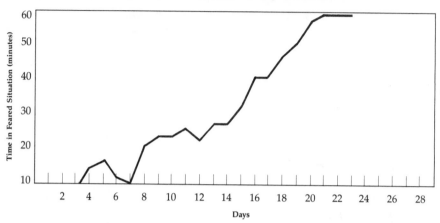

they are anticipated. With each effort, the spouse should give positive feedback. When the patient achieves less than before, support for trying again and an understanding of the effort involved are needed. Once a meaningful amount of gain has been made, the newfound skills should be repeatedly practiced; the best way to do this is to incorporate whatever gains are made into everyday life. This will often demand that the spouse relinquish some household responsibility or encourage new social behavior in the patient. The ultimate aim should be to undertake regular activities outside the home; and the best of these for the agoraphobic is a job.

When panic strikes in the presence of the spouse, it is important that he or she behave in a way that minimizes the effects of anxiety. The best way for the spouse to help the panic victim is to first find a place to sit down, as near to the scene that provoked the panic as possible. Second, do not discuss the symptoms that are being experienced at the time; such attention to symptoms will tend to make them worse. Sit with your spouse until the symptoms dissipate. This will usually take only a few minutes. As the panic dies down, talk about some neutral topic, and when the attack is fully over, suggest a visit to the place in which panic occurred so that the experience does not lead to further avoidance.

Remember that exposure practice may have to last for several months, during which a daily practice schedule leading to steadily increasing mobility should be encouraged. Should relapse occur, immediately resume exposure practice; do not wait until all the symptoms reappear. At the first sign of decreasing mobility start the practice in confronting the phobic situation once again.

Confrontation of feared situations is not only curative, it can prevent relapse. Ultimately, the agoraphobic and spouse need to live a fuller life, without restriction of activity. Such a fuller life demands constant attention and careful continued planning. But the rewards are surely worth the effort!

■

The viewpoint of scientists as they investigate a particular problem is affected by the concerns of the time. Sometimes this leads to tunnel vision. In the early days of behavior therapy the focus was upon observable behavior—a legacy of the animal laboratory and an antidote to the less scientific approach of psychoanalysis. The prevailing view was that phobic behavior, like other behaviors, was learned and could therefore be unlearned. As we have seen, this approach paid off with the development of more effective behavior-change procedures. Panic, however, was ignored by behavioral scientists. At the same time, those pursuing a pharmacological approach concentrated upon panic but tended to ignore the contribution of learning to the development and treatment of panic. Their work was informed by the view that panic is a result of a biological perturbation of the central nervous system. Again, the approach paid off, and effective pharmacological agents were discovered.

The development of systematic desensitization, which led to exposure therapy, and the discovery of the effectiveness of antidepressants in the treatment of the panic syndrome have created a dramatic improvement in our ability to treat both simple phobias and the more complex agoraphobic state. The identification of exposure to the feared situation as the core of all psychotherapeutic approaches has allowed us to simplify the treatment of fears and phobias.

We have seen that the once separate approaches of biology and learning now merge at two levels—in certain processes in the brain cell, where learning seems to affect chemical control systems; and in external behavior, where the combination of drugs and exposure therapy has proven most effective in treating the agoraphobic with panic. An understanding of the interaction between learning and biology is essential to the further unraveling of both the cause and cure of phobias and panic. It is in this area that unresolved questions still exist, and these questions will form the focus for research in the immediate future. Such questions include the precise actions of medication: Do medications specifically block panic, or are they more general anti-anxiety compounds? What is the best combination of therapies over the long term? Are the benefits of more complex therapies worth the increased expense to the patient? Are medications useful in the treatment of social phobia, a problem still relatively ignored? In broad terms, these questions resolve into a search for refinements of treatment along lines that have already been established.

More basic work in both psychology and neurochemistry is needed to throw further light upon the learning and chemical control of fear and the nature of panic. The chemical processes accompanying learning need to be further uncovered. We need a more complete grasp of the mechanisms underlying long-term maintenance of new behaviors so that we can help patients to maintain their gains. The isolation of the natural anxiety-provoking or anxiety-reducing substances might lead to the formulation of new pharmacological compounds, in time, and to new and more effective treatment approaches.

The ultimate question is, Can the panic syndrome and phobias be prevented? For it is prevention, not treatment, that provides the best hope for the future. A first step in addressing this question is, as it has been in other areas of medicine, to identify the factors conferring a high risk for developing these conditions. We have seen that some risk factors have been identified, although the relative strength of their contribution to the disorders has not been established. Factors enhancing the risk of developing the panic syndrome include a family history of phobia, panic, and depression. School phobia may be a risk factor for the development of a later panic syndrome. Other risk factors need to be identified if we are going to be able to spot those persons at risk of developing disabling phobias.

Would the ability to identify a group of individuals, preferably in childhood, who are at high risk of developing phobias with or without panic, enable us to prevent the emergence of these disorders? One approach would be to help the family to expose these children in a systematic way to separation experiences and to other fear-provoking situations, thus overcoming avoidance behavior at an early age.

We may be many years away from testing such prevention programs and the eventual reduction of the number of cases of phobia and panic in the population of the United States. And even if we reach such a goal, might not future lifestyle changes bring about another increase in the prevalence of the disorder?

Clifford Simak, in his short story of the future, "Huddling Place," written in 1944, suggests one such scenario.

> Webster huddled back into his chair again, feeling desolate and alone and misplaced. Alone in a humming lobby that pulsed with life—a loneliness that tore at him, that left him limp and weak.
>
> Homesickness. Downright, shameful homesickness, he told himself. Something that boys are supposed to feel when they first go out to meet the world. There was a fancy name for it—agoraphobia.
>
> If he crossed the room to the television booth (and called home) . . . perhaps it would help. Not much, maybe, but some. He started to rise from the chair again and froze. The few short steps to the booth held terror, a terrible overwhelming terror. If he crossed them, he would have to run. Run to escape the watching eyes, the unfamiliar sounds, the agonizing nearness of strange faces.[16]

With the advent of the computer it is already possible to work at home and communicate with the office. Future developments, such as video-communication systems, might allow most people to live and work within a small radius of their home. With this environmental constriction, if faced with the necessity of a journey, would they conform to Simak's vision of the future?

Such a scenario may be merely a fantasy, but it serves to remind us that changes in our environment affect and may even determine the disorders with which we are afflicted. Factors in our environment may influence disease far more, for better or worse, than improvements in medical treatment. Clean water, better housing, and adequate nutrition—all a result of the Industrial Revolution and the consequent generally improved standard of living—dramatically reduced the death rate from infectious disease. But later, this now affluent society, able to afford the automobile and thus reduce exercise, and able to purchase rich fatty foods, has been afflicted by epidemics of heart disease and automobile accidents. None of this was predictable from the knowledge available at the time these changes were taking place.

At this very moment changes in lifestyle—particularly in the role of women—may be altering the nature of agoraphobia. Over the last decade, measures of phobic behavior in participants enrolled in our studies have revealed that the limitation of mobility associated with agoraphobia is diminishing with time. In an earlier chapter, we saw that females are more fearful than males, and attributed this to differences in social conditioning: Little boys are taught to be brave, while little girls are allowed to express fear and dependence in anxiety-provoking situations. While this early differential treatment of children may or may not be changing, notable changes are occurring in the lives of adult women. Only a few years ago men worked outside the home, while women's work was usually confined to the home. Today women are working outside the home—both for personal fulfillment and from economic necessity.

Three brief case histories illustrate the effects of the expansion of women's roles. The first patient is almost totally housebound; only occasionally does she venture outside her home—and then always accompanied by her husband. Her husband and her children manage the grocery shopping. Her social life is dependent upon the telephone and visits from friends, and for entertainment she depends upon the television set. This woman does not have to work to augment the family income; hers is the traditional role of the housewife. Because of her limitations others perform critical tasks for her, so that she has little incentive to change.

The second patient must shoulder her share of the family budget. She leaves home and drives to and from work each day along the same "safe" route. Financial necessity and her pleasure in her work—she holds a responsible position—enable her to endure the panic attacks she experiences during the workday. Upon returning home from work she retires to her room. She has not visited the kitchen for months; her husband and children prepare the meals and do the household chores. Were it not for her need to work, this woman would, like our first patient, be housebound; she is certainly disabled in her role of homemaker. As it is, her automobile has become an extension of her room; the moment she opens her car door to get out she feels shaky.

The last of the trio lives by herself. Housebound for several years, changes in her life forced her to live alone and to fend for herself. She is now almost fully recovered; only the need to take a long journey without a companion would trouble her. As she puts it, "I have to earn a living, so I must drive to work. If I don't do the shopping I'll starve; no one else will do it for me." Economic necessity, and the lack of anyone to free her of essential tasks, have together eradicated her phobic limitation by forcing exposure to her feared situations.

These three women illustrate the more general observation that the increasing tendency of women to join the work force tends to diminish agoraphobic limitation; we see social and economic forces fostering therapeutic gains. Agoraphobia is still more frequent in women than in men, but it will be interesting to follow the relative distribution of agoraphobia between the sexes over the next few years. One's reason for engaging in exposure—whether as part of therapy, or because of the effects of social change—is not the crucial factor in achieving relief. As we have seen, it is the amount of exposure that counts. The changing social environment may be reducing the degree of phobic limitation by forcing a greater degree of exposure.

While we don't know whether fears, phobias, and panic will increase or decrease in the future, we do know that our ability to influence either the long-term messages transmitted by genes, or the shorter-term messages from the environment that we call experience, will ultimately determine the numbers. Rarely does a major research finding dramatically alter the treatment of a disease. More commonly it is the careful building of one study upon another, and the transfer of findings in the basic sciences to the clinical situation, followed by clinical research, that leads to progress. All this may seem too slow to those we cannot help effectively today, but it is the only sure way to proceed toward our goal of overcoming useless fear.

Overcoming our fears, phobias, and anxieties is part of our personal and communal commitment to reaching our full human potential. As a society we must continue to tackle the fascinating problem of how to control the harmful aspects of the fear response while retaining its protective benefits. At a personal level, we can grow by recognizing and confronting our fears instead of hiding them from ourselves and from others. By our concerted efforts we can reduce the dreadful toll of fear imposed upon so many people today.

NOTES

1. William Hoffer, *Saved!* (New York: Bantam Books, 1980).
2. L. Salzman, "Obsessions and Phobia." Paper presented to the International Forum of Psychoanalysis, Zurich, Switzerland, 1965.
3. In many cases mitral valve prolapse will not require treatment. Some individuals with mitral valve prolapse have a heart rate higher than normal; this can be treated with a beta-blocker, a drug that slows the heart rate. Although such drugs may also diminish some of the symptoms of anxiety such as tremulous hands, they have not been found useful in the treatment of panic disorder. A regular exercise program will also help slow the heart and promote cardiovascular fitness.
4. Charles R. Darwin, *The Expression of the Emotions in Men and Animals* (New York: Appleton and Company, 1897).
5. G. Stanley Hall, "A Study of Fears," *American Journal of Psychology* 8 (1897): 150–247.
6. A. T. Jersild and F. B. Holmes, "Children's Fears," *Child Development Monograph* 20 (1935).
7. Sigmund Freud, *Collected Papers*, vol. 3 (London: Hogarth Press, 1950).
8. J. B. Watson, "Conditioned Emotional Reflexes," *Journal of Experimental Psychology* 3 (1920): 1–23.
9. L. Eisenberg, "School Phobia: A Study in the Communication of Anxiety," *American Journal of Psychology* 114 (1958): 712–718.
10. Mary Cover Jones, "The Elimination of Children's Fears," *Journal of Experimental Psychology* 7 (1924): 328–390.
11. Joseph Wolpe, "Psychotherapy by Reciprocal Inhibition," *Journal of Experimental Psychology* 7 (1924): 382–390.
12. P. J. Lang and D. A. Lazovik, "The Experimental Desensitization of a Phobia," *Journal of Abnormal and Social Psychology* 66 (1963): 519–525.
13. D. F. Klein and J. Rabkin, eds., *Anxiety: New Research and Changing Concepts* (New York: Raven Press, 1981).
14. Clomipramine appears to be the most effective medication for compulsions, but it is not presently available in the United States. Until it has been approved, other antidepressants may be prescribed.
15. See the second reference (Bower and Bower) in the list of suggested readings for more detailed information concerning assertiveness.
16. Clifford D. Simak, "Huddling Place," in Isaac Asimov and Martin Greenberg, eds., *The Golden Years of Science Fiction* (New York: Bonanza Books, 1984).

SUGGESTED READING

Bandura, A. *Social Learning Theory.* Englewood Cliffs, NJ: Prentice-Hall, 1977. An excellent introduction to modern learning theory, and to social influences upon human development and behavior change.

Bower, S. A. and G. H. Bower. *Asserting Yourself: A Practical Guide for Positive Change.* New York: Addison-Wesley, 1976. Combines a do-it-yourself guide of particular relevance to the social phobic with an excellent description of assertiveness.

Freud, S. *New Introductory Lectures in Psychoanalysis.* New York: W. W. Norton, 1961. An overview of psychoanalytic theory and principles by the founder of the field.

Leavitt, F. *Drugs and Behavior.* 2d ed. New York: John Wiley and Sons, 1982. This book introduces the reader to the research methods and major findings of modern psychopharmacology.

Ornstein, R. and R. F. Thompson. *The Amazing Brain.* Boston: Houghton Mifflin, 1984. An introduction, written in an easily understandable manner, to the structure and function of the brain.

Schwartz, B. and H. Lacey. *Behaviorism, Science, and Human Nature.* New York: W. W. Norton, 1982. An overview of the theoretical basis and the findings of studies of conditioning.

Skinner, B. F. *Science and Human Behavior.* New York: Macmillan, 1953. A basic description of the science of psychology, its findings, and its applications for the social good from the perspective of Skinner's psychological theories.

Stern, R. and W. J. Ray. *Psychophysiological Recording.* New York: Oxford University Press, 1980. An introduction to the methods used in physiological assessment and an overview of basic physiological mechanisms.

Wolpe, J. *The Practice of Behavior Therapy.* 3d ed. New York: Pergamon Press, 1982. Particularly valuable for its chapters on systematic desensitization by the physician who introduced the procedure.

ABOUT THE AUTHOR

Stewart Agras, professor of psychiatry and behavioral science at Stanford University Medical School, has been interested in phobias from the beginning of his medical career. His first published paper, on the subject of school phobia, marked the beginning of his outstanding contributions to the development of behavior therapy. As director of the Behavioral Medicine Program at Stanford he continues, in his clinical work, teaching, and research, to explore the problems of panic and phobia and, more recently, of eating disorders.

His research on the application of basic psychological findings to the clinical situation has brought Dr. Agras to the forefront of his specialty during the last twenty-five years. He has served as president of the Society of Behavioral Medicine, and was recently elected president of the Association for the Advancement of Behavior Therapy—the only physician to hold both these positions. The author of nearly 150 scientific papers and two books, he has also served as editor of the *Journal of Applied Behavioral Analysis*.

English by birth, Stewart Agras has had a broad experience of the North American continent. After receiving his M.D. from London University, he completed his residency and fellowship at McGill University in Montreal, where he also taught. He joined the faculty of the University of Vermont College of Medicine in 1961, in 1969 went to the University of Mississippi Medical Center as chairman of the Psychiatry Department, and has been at Stanford since 1973.

Series Editor: Miriam Miller
Production Manager: Laura Ackerman-Shaw
Cover and Book Design: Andrew Danish
Illustrations: Jim McGuinness

INDEX

Calcium, 54, 60
Cancer: in panic victims, 17, 18 (table)
Cats, fear of, 21, 23 (table), 117, 125
Ceraunophobia (fear of lightning), 23 (table)
Cerebral cortex, 59, 61
Checking ritual, 25, 85
Children's fears, 19, 29, 34, 70; treatment of, 124–125; *see also* School phobia; Separation fears
Circulatory diseases: in panic victims, 17, 18 (table)
Civil War, 15
Classification of phobias, 21–13; table, 23
Claustrophobia (fear of enclosed places), *see* Enclosed places
Clomipramine, 101
Common fears, 1f, 32–34; vs. simple phobias, 2–3, 23, 34, 64, 117f; functions, 4, 18f, 33; studies of, 28–29, 33f; major categories of, 32; sex differences, 32–33; development of, 33 (fig.); treatment of, 124–25. *See also* Children's fears; *and individual feared objects by name*
Complex phobias, 3, 120, 122, 126–28
Compulsive behavior and rituals, 3, 25–26; frequency, 28; treatment, 85–89, 101, 127–28
"Conditioned Emotional Reactions" (Watson; 1919), 43
Conditioning, 43–49, 60–64, 70f
Contamination, fear of, 23 (table), 25–26. *See also* Handwashing ritual
Crowds, fear of, 28
Curiosity: and fear response, 30
Cynophobia (fear of dogs), *see* Dogs

Darkness, fear of, 23, (table), 28f
Darwin, Charles, 23
Death, fear of, 28f, 36
Dendrite, 54
Dentists, fear of, 31 (table)
Depression, 18, 26, 38f, 64; link to agoraphobia-panic syndrome, 9, 12, 38–39, 101, 135; and compulsive behavior, 101, 128
Descartes, René, 21
Desensitization, 70–77, 90–91, 133; recovery rates, 73–75

Desynchrony, 93
Disease, fear of, 29. *See also* Handwashing ritual
Dogs, fear of, 23 (table), 99, 117, 125
Double-blind drug studies, 98
Drug addiction, 18
Drug therapy, 4, 56–58, 93, 97f, 103, 105, 129, 134

Echocardiography, 15
Enclosed places, fear of, 3, 23 (table), 31 (table), 34, 46, 50–51, 73, 82, 119, 122
Enzyme action in neurochemistry, 56
Equinophobia (fear of horses), *see* Horses
Exposure therapy, 83–92, 101–3, 124f; for compulsive behavior, 80, 128; pain of, 90, 107–10; as core treatment for fears and phobias, 112–13, 128–29, 132–33; parent-assisted for children's fears, 124–25; daily practice in, 125, 129–133
"Extinction burst," 81

"Fainting spells," 9
Families: and compulsive members, 26, 128; phobic patterns in, 37f. *See also* Marital relationships; Social transmission of phobias
Fear response: biological role, 23, 30, 59, 63; stimuli provoking, 48–51; and nervous system, 59, 62; beneficial and harmful effects of, 63, 137
Fears, acquisition of, 64. *See also* Children's fears; Common fears
Fears and phobias, self-assessment of, 121 (table), 123 (fig.)
Female fears and phobias, *see* Sex differences
Fire, fear of, 23 (table)
Flying, fear of, 2, 31 (table), 119, 126
Frequency of phobias, 9, 27–28
Freud, Sigmund, 41–43, 83
Frog phobia (case study), 22

Gamma aminobutyric acid (GABA), 58–59
Group therapy: efficacy of, 74, 108, 109–10

Hall, G. Stanley, 28–29, 33; 1897 study, 29
Handwashing ritual, 25, 85, 87–89
Heart disease: in panic victims, 17
Heart rate: and activity, 12 (fig.); in panic attacks, 13–14, 100; and anxiety, 15, 58; in exposure therapy, 91–92 (figs.)
Heart rhythm: in panic attack, 13
Heights, fear of, 3, 22–34, 73, 84, 99, 118, 122, 126; frequency, 28, 31 (tables)
Heredity: and fears, 21, 37
High blood pressure: in anxiety victims, 17
Hippocrates, 21
Horses, fear of, 23 (table), 41–43
"Huddling Place" (Simak; 1944), 135
Hypochondriasis, see Injury and illness
"Hysterical vertigo," 9

Imipramine, 97ff, 104f, 129
Implosion therapy, 84f, 90
Incidence of phobias, 9, 27–28
Industrial Revolution, 136
Injury and illness, fear of, 3, 28, 31 (table), 32, 35, 63, 120, 122; rate, 31 (table); case studies, 80–91
Insects, fear of, 117–18. See also Spiders
Institute of Psychiatry (London), 84
Isolation: link to panic syndrome, 9, 12. See also Depression

James I, king of England, 21
Jersild and Holmes study (mid-1930s), 29
Jones, Mary Cover, 68, 70f

Kinsey study, 29
Klein, Donald, 95–98

Lang, Peter, 74
Learning and biology, 60–61. See also Biological-psychological interaction
Librium, 57. See also Benzodiazepines
Limitations: as disabling effect of phobias, 1f, 9, 11
"Little Albert" case (Watson; 1919), 43–45, 51, 60, 71, 96
"Little Hans" case (Freud; 1909), 41–43

Male fears and phobias, see Sex differences
Marital relationships: and agoraphobia-panic syndrome, 110–15, 130, 132. See also Families
Marplan, 129
Memories: role in fear/phobia repsonses, 50–51, 64
Merchant of Venice, The (Shakespeare), 21
"Mini-phobia" experiments, 49–50, 60–61
Minnesota Multiphasic Personality Inventory (MMPI), 73
Mitral valve prolapse, 15, 16 (fig.)
Mobility, 1, 9, 11, 18, 79–81, 120, 136–37
Monamine oxidase inhibitors, 129
Mortality rates: in panic victims, 17f
Myophobia (fear of contamination), see Contamination

Nardil, 129
Nature-nurture arguments, 18, 37–39
Neurochemistry, 4, 54–61, 133–34. See also Drug therapy
Neurons, 53–54
Neuroses: defined, 17, 26; historic views of, 42, 95
Neurotransmitters, 54, 55 (fig.), 58, 60–61, 64
New York State Psychiatric Institute, 95
Nyctophobia (fear of darkness), see Darkness

"Old" and "new" brain, 59
Open spaces, fear of, see Agoraphobia
Ophidiophobia (fear of snakes), see Snakes

Panic attacks, 3–9, 14 (fig.), 24, 100, 114, 129, 130, 132; symptoms, 9–11, 120; spontaneous, 13, 96; and fear of separation, 95–96, 98; treatment, 103, 104–5, 129, 130; precipitating factors, 120. See also Agoraphobia; Panic syndrome
Panic syndrome: defined, 3, 19; frequency, 8, 28; features, 8–11; and diseases, 16–17; mortality rate of victims, 17; biological influences, 17,